# Topical Bible

# for Kids

## ESV

by

Michelle Brock

# Kids!

This book is for you.

There are a lot of great Bible verses that will help you and encourage you. If you don't find a topic you are looking for, then make your own list! There is room in the back of the book for your own Bible topic lists.

P.S. There are some notes for parents in the back of the book, too!

# Table of Contents

# AFRAID

Related topics: Worry, Trust, Confidence

When I am afraid, I put my trust in you. In God, whose word I praise, in God I trust; I shall not be afraid. What can flesh do to me? Psalm 56:3-4

**Praying helps me when I am afraid.**
"And call upon me in the day of trouble; I will deliver you, and you shall glorify me." Psalm 50:15

**Because God is all powerful, I can ask him to help me when I am afraid.**
God is our refuge and strength, a very present help in trouble. Psalm 46:1

Fear not, for I am with you; be not dismayed, for I am your God; I will strengthen you, I will help you, I will uphold you with my righteous right hand. Isaiah 41:10

From the end of the earth I call to you when my heart is faint. Lead me to the rock that is higher than I, for you have been my refuge, a strong tower against the enemy. Psalm 61:2-3

**Because God takes care of me, I can sleep and not be afraid in the dark.**
In peace I will both lie down and sleep; for you alone, O LORD, make me dwell in safety. Psalm 4:8

**I learn to trust God when I remember that he is a Good Shepherd who loves me.**

I am the good shepherd. I know my own. John 10:14a

The LORD is my shepherd; I shall not want. He makes me lie down in green pastures. He leads me beside still waters. He restores my soul. He leads me in paths of righteousness for his name's sake. Even though I walk through the valley of the shadow of death, I will fear no evil, for you are with me; your rod and your staff, they comfort me. Psalm 23:1-4

**Wisdom helps me to stop being fearful at bedtime.**

My son, do not lose sight of these—keep sound wisdom and discretion, and they will be life for your soul and adornment for your neck. Then you will walk on your way securely, and your foot will not stumble. If you lie down, you will not be afraid; when you lie down, your sleep will be sweet. Proverbs 3:21-24

**Because storms obey God, I can trust him during thunderstorms!**

And a great windstorm arose, and the waves were breaking into the boat, so that the boat was already filling. But he was in the stern, asleep on the cushion. And they woke him and said to him, "Teacher, do you not care that we are perishing?" And he awoke and rebuked the wind and said to the sea, "Peace! Be still!" And the wind ceased, and there was a great calm. Mark 4:37-39

**I can pray for boldness (even when I am afraid) like the first Christians.**

"And now, Lord, look upon their threats and grant to your servants to continue to speak your word with all boldness, while you stretch out your hand to heal, and signs and wonders are performed through the name of your holy servant Jesus." And when they had prayed, the place in which they were gathered together was shaken, and they were all filled with the Holy Spirit and continued to speak the word of God with boldness. Acts 4:29-31

**Because God made me, he knows all about my weaknesses and can help me.**

But Moses said to the LORD, "Oh, my Lord, I am not eloquent, either in the past or since you have spoken to your servant, but I am slow of speech and of tongue." Then the LORD said to him, "Who has made man's mouth? Who makes him mute, or deaf, or seeing, or blind? Is it not I, the LORD? Now therefore go, and I will be with your mouth and teach you what you shall speak." Exodus 4:10-12

He who calls you is faithful; he will surely do it. 1 Thessalonians 5:24

The LORD will fulfill his purpose for me; your steadfast love, O LORD, endures forever. Do not forsake the work of your hands. Psalm 138:8

> Elijah's servant was afraid until he realized that God was more powerful than his enemies. 2 Kings 6:15-23 (See Psalm 34:7)
>
> Asa was a king who was afraid of a big army, and he prayed for help. God delivered him because he relied on God's help. 2 Chronicles 14:11-12

# ANGER

Related topics: Patience, Forgiveness, Humility, Selfish

**Anger can come from selfish desires.**

For the anger of man does not produce the righteousness of God. James 1:20

Whoever is slow to anger is better than the mighty, and he who rules his spirit than he who takes a city. Proverbs 16:32

It is better to live in a desert land than with a quarrelsome and fretful woman. Proverbs 21:19

Make no friendship with a man given to anger, nor go with a wrathful man, lest you learn his ways and entangle yourself in a snare. Proverbs 22:24-25

**Because God forgave me, I am learning to be kind and forgiving instead of angry.**
A soft answer turns away wrath, but a harsh word stirs up anger. The tongue of the wise commends knowledge, but the mouths of fools pour out folly. Proverbs 15:1-2

Let all bitterness and wrath and anger and clamor and slander be put away from you, along with all malice. Be kind to one another, tenderhearted, forgiving one another, as God in Christ forgave you. Ephesians 4:31-32

**I can be slow to anger by learning to ask questions instead of talking, and then listening to the answers.**
Know this, my beloved brothers: let every person be quick to hear, slow to speak, slow to anger; James 1:19

**Impatience that comes from pride often leads to anger.**
Better is the end of a thing than its beginning, and the patient in spirit is better than the proud in spirit. Be not quick in your spirit to become angry, for anger lodges in the bosom of fools. Ecclesiastes 7:8-9

**I learn patience by learning to trust God.**
Be still before the LORD and wait patiently for him; fret not yourself over the one who prospers in his way, over the man who carries out evil devices! Psalm 37:7

Refrain from anger, and forsake wrath! Fret not yourself; it tends only to evil. For the evildoers shall be cut off, but those who wait for the LORD shall inherit the land. Psalm 37:8-9

Balaam was angry with his donkey. He didn't know God used his donkey to protect him. Numbers 22:21-35 (Sometimes I am angry when I don't get my own way, and I forget that God uses my circumstances for good.)

Jonah was angry because God forgave people he hated. Jonah 4:1-4

# BAPTISM

**Jesus wants his disciples to be baptized.**

And Jesus came and said to them, "All authority in heaven and on earth has been given to me. Go therefore and make disciples of all nations, baptizing them in the name of the Father and of the Son and of the Holy Spirit, teaching them to observe all that I have commanded you. And behold, I am with you always, to the end of the age." Matthew 28:18-20

**Christians are baptized after they are saved.**

But when they believed Philip as he preached good news about the kingdom of God and the name of Jesus Christ, they were baptized, both men and women. Acts 8:12

And as they were going along the road they came to some water, and the eunuch said, "See, here is water! What prevents me from being baptized?" And he commanded the chariot to stop, and they both went down into the water, Philip and the eunuch, and he baptized him. And when they came up out of the water, the Spirit of the Lord carried Philip away, and the eunuch saw him no more, and went on his way rejoicing. Acts 8:36, 38-39

**Baptism is how the first Christians began to be a part of a local church.**

So those who received his word were baptized, and there were added that day about three thousand souls. And they devoted themselves to the apostles' teaching and the fellowship, to the breaking of bread and the prayers.  Acts 2:41-42

**Baptism is a way of telling the story of the gospel, and telling others that Jesus has saved us, and that we want to follow him.**

Do you not know that all of us who have been baptized into Christ Jesus were baptized into his death? We were buried therefore with him by baptism into death, in order that, just as Christ was raised from the dead by the glory of the Father, we too might walk in newness of life. For if we have been united with him in a death like his, we shall certainly be united with him in a resurrection like his. Romans 6:3-5

> Jesus set an example for me when he was baptized. Matthew 3:13-17

# Beauty

**The Bible tells me that God is beautiful! Everything else that is beautiful is like him!**
One thing have I asked of the LORD, that will I seek after: that I may dwell in the house of the LORD all the days of my life, to gaze upon the beauty of the LORD and to inquire in his temple. Psalm 27:4

**God will make everything beautiful when he is ready, including me!**
He has made everything beautiful in its time. Ecclesiastes 3:11a

**Outside beauty is not nearly as important as the beauty of loving and fearing God!**
Charm is deceitful, and beauty is vain, but a woman who fears the LORD is to be praised. Give her of the fruit of her hands, and let her works praise her in the gates. Proverbs 31:30-31

But the LORD said to Samuel, "Do not look on his appearance or on the height of his stature, because I have rejected him. For the LORD sees not as man sees: man looks on the outward appearance, but the LORD looks on the heart." 1 Samuel 16:7

**God loves the beauty of a gentle and quiet spirit!**
But let your adorning be the hidden person of the heart with the imperishable beauty of a gentle and quiet spirit, which in God's sight is very precious. 1 Peter 3:4

**God makes attractive people. It's all mixed up if those people aren't attractive inside, too.**
Like a gold ring in a pig's snout is a beautiful woman without discretion. Proverbs 11:22

A
B
C
D
E
F
G
H
I
J
K
L
M
N
O
P
Q
R
S
T
U
V
W
X
Y
Z

### Holiness is beautiful!

Ascribe to the LORD the glory due his name; worship the LORD in the splendor of holiness. Psalm 29:2

### Salvation is beautiful!

I will greatly rejoice in the LORD; my soul shall exult in my God, for he has clothed me with the garments of salvation; he has covered me with the robe of righteousness, as a bridegroom decks himself like a priest with a beautiful headdress, and as a bride adorns herself with her jewels. Isaiah 61:10

As it is written, "How beautiful are the feet of those who preach the good news!" Romans 10:15b

Can a virgin forget her ornaments, or a bride her attire? Yet my people have forgotten me days without number. Jeremiah 2:32

# BIBLE STUDY

**The Bible shows me my motives and what God wants me to change.**

For the word of God is living and active, sharper than any two-edged sword, piercing to the division of soul and of spirit, of joints and of marrow, and discerning the thoughts and intentions of the heart. Hebrews 4:12

**Even a child who cannot read well can obey what he knows is true.**

For Ezra had set his heart to study the Law of the LORD, and to do it and to teach his statutes and rules in Israel. Ezra 7:10

**I like to think about the Bible.**

Your words were found, and I ate them, and your words became to me a joy and the delight of my heart, for I am called by your name, O LORD, God of hosts. Jeremiah 15:16

Your testimonies are my delight; they are my counselors. Psalm 119:24

I will meditate on your precepts and fix my eyes on your ways. I will delight in your statutes; I will not forget your word. Psalm 119:15-16

**I want to learn to understand and love the Bible.**

But his delight is in the law of the LORD, and on his law he meditates day and night. He is like a tree planted by streams of water that yields its fruit in its season, and its leaf does not wither. In all that he does, he prospers. Psalm 1:2-3

Praise the LORD! Blessed is the man who fears the LORD, who greatly delights in his commandments! Psalm 112:1

Knowing this first of all, that no prophecy of Scripture comes from someone's own interpretation. For no prophecy was ever produced by the will of man, but men spoke from God as they were carried along by the Holy Spirit. 2 Peter 1:20-21

**The Holy Spirit uses the Bible to teach God's children.**

And take the helmet of salvation, and the sword of the Spirit, which is the word of God, Ephesians 6:17

**Some things in the Bible are hard to understand, even for adults!**

And count the patience of our Lord as salvation, just as our beloved brother Paul also wrote to you according to the wisdom given him, as he does in all his letters when he speaks in them of these matters. There are some things in them that are hard to understand, which the ignorant and unstable twist to their own destruction, as they do the other Scriptures. 2 Peter 3:15-16

Psalm 119 is the longest chapter in the Bible, and it is all about the Bible. See if you can find all the different words King David used to refer to the Bible.

# BIRDS

## God uses birds to teach me what he is like!

But they who wait for the LORD shall renew their strength; they shall mount up with wings like eagles; they shall run and not be weary; they shall walk and not faint. Isaiah 40:31

Are not two sparrows sold for a penny? And not one of them will fall to the ground apart from your Father. But even the hairs of your head are all numbered. Fear not, therefore; you are of more value than many sparrows. Matthew 10:29-31

"Is it by your understanding that the hawk soars and spreads his wings toward the south? Is it at your command that the eagle mounts up and makes his nest on high? On the rock he dwells and makes his home, on the rocky crag and stronghold. From there he spies out the prey; his eyes behold it from far away. His young ones suck up blood, and where the slain are, there is he." Job 39:26-30

Look at the birds of the air: they neither sow nor reap nor gather into barns, and yet your heavenly Father feeds them. Are you not of more value than they? But seek first the kingdom of God and his righteousness, and all these things will be added to you. Matthew 6:26, 33

He who dwells in the shelter of the Most High will abide in the shadow of the Almighty. I will say to the LORD, "My refuge and my fortress, my God, in whom I trust." For he will deliver you from the snare of the fowler and from the deadly pestilence. He will cover you with his pinions, and under his wings you will find refuge; his faithfulness is a shield and buckler. Psalm 91:1-4

Bless the LORD, O my soul, and forget not all his benefits, who forgives all your iniquity, who heals all your diseases, who redeems your life from the pit, who crowns you with steadfast love and mercy, who satisfies you with good so that your youth is renewed like the eagle's. Psalm 103:2-5

Sing to the LORD with thanksgiving; make melody to our God on the lyre! He covers the heavens with clouds; he prepares rain for the earth; he makes grass grow on the hills. He gives to the beasts their food, and to the young ravens that cry. Psalm 147:7-9

# Bullies

Related topic: Mean People

**God sees when I am mistreated.**

"Whoever receives one such child in my name receives me, but whoever causes one of these little ones who believe in me to sin, it would be better for him to have a great millstone fastened around his neck and to be drowned in the depth of the sea." Matthew 18:5-6

**God will help me not be silent when I see someone being bullied.**

Open your mouth, judge righteously, defend the rights of the poor and needy. Proverbs 31:9

Learn to do good; seek justice, correct oppression; bring justice to the fatherless, plead the widow's cause. Isaiah 1:17

"Give counsel; grant justice; make your shade like night at the height of noon; shelter the outcasts; do not reveal the fugitive; let the outcasts of Moab sojourn among you; be a shelter to them from the destroyer." Isaiah 16:3-4a

**I can follow Jesus' example to help those who are weaker than I am.**

We who are strong have an obligation to bear with the failings of the weak, and not to please ourselves. Let each of us please his neighbor for his good, to build him up. For Christ did not please himself, but as it is written, "The reproaches of those who reproached you fell on me." Romans 15:1-3

For you have been a stronghold to the poor, a stronghold to the needy in his distress, a shelter from the storm and a shade from the heat; for the breath of the ruthless is like a storm against a wall. Isaiah 25:4

Light dawns in the darkness for the upright; he is gracious, merciful, and righteous. Psalm 112:4

A
B
C
D
E
F
G
H
I
J
K
L
M
N
O
P
Q
R
S
T
U
V
W
X
Y
Z

**God wants me to tell someone in authority when someone is trying to hurt me or someone else.**

Now the son of Paul's sister heard of their ambush, so he went and entered the barracks and told Paul. Paul called one of the centurions and said, "Take this young man to the tribune, for he has something to tell him." Acts 23:16-17

**God wants me to pray for bullies.**

"You have heard that it was said, 'You shall love your neighbor and hate your enemy.' But I say to you, Love your enemies and pray for those who persecute you, so that you may be sons of your Father who is in heaven. For he makes his sun rise on the evil and on the good, and sends rain on the just and on the unjust." Matthew 5:43-45

**God does not want me to "get back at" bullies, or take revenge when I am wronged.**

Beloved, never avenge yourselves, but leave it to the wrath of God, for it is written, "Vengeance is mine, I will repay, says the Lord." To the contrary, "if your enemy is hungry, feed him; if he is thirsty, give him something to drink; for by so doing you will heap burning coals on his head." Do not be overcome by evil, but overcome evil with good.
Romans 12:19-21

King David wrote Psalm 35 when he was dealing with enemies.

# CHILDREN

Even a child makes himself known by his acts, by whether his conduct is pure and upright. Proverbs 20:11

### Jesus loves to hear me talk to him.

Then children were brought to him that he might lay his hands on them and pray. The disciples rebuked the people, but Jesus said, "Let the little children come to me and do not hinder them, for to such belongs the kingdom of heaven." And he laid his hands on them and went away. Matthew 19:13-15

### God can use me by my example to others.

Let no one despise you for your youth, but set the believers an example in speech, in conduct, in love, in faith, in purity. 1 Timothy 4:12

### God's Word is for children, too!

Assemble the people, men, women, and little ones, and the sojourner within your towns, that they may hear and learn to fear the LORD your God, and be careful to do all the words of this law. Deuteronomy 31:12

"The secret things belong to the LORD our God, but the things that are revealed belong to us and to our children forever, that we may do all the words of this law." Deuteronomy 29:29

> Timothy learned the Bible as a child, and stayed faithful as an adult! 2 Timothy 3:14-17
>
> Jesus reminded the people that God's truth is spoken by children! Matthew 21:15-16

A
B
C
D
E
F
G
H
I
J
K
L
M
N
O
P
Q
R
S
T
U
V
W
X
Y
Z

# CHORES

Related topic: Work

**God wants me to be a good steward, and learn to take care of my things.**
But all things should be done decently and in order.
1 Corinthians 14:40

Know well the condition of your flocks, and give attention to your herds. Proverbs 27:23

Whoever is slothful will not roast his game, but the diligent man will get precious wealth. Proverbs 12:27

Moreover, it is required of stewards that they be found trustworthy. 1 Corinthians 4:2

And he said to him, 'Well done, good servant! Because you have been faithful in a very little, you shall have authority over ten cities.' Luke 19:17

So, whether you eat or drink, or whatever you do, do all to the glory of God. 1 Corinthians 10:31

**I am encouraged when I remember that God will reward my hard work.**
And let us not grow weary of doing good, for in due season we will reap, if we do not give up. Galatians 6:9

Whatever you do, work heartily, as for the Lord and not for men. Colossians 3:23

**God wants me to work so that I can do good for others.**
"In all things I have shown you that by working hard in this way we must help the weak and remember the words of the Lord Jesus, how he himself said, 'It is more blessed to give than to receive.'" Acts 20:35

# COMPLAINING

Related topics: Thankfulness, Contentment

Do all things without grumbling or questioning [arguing], Philippians 2:14

Nor grumble, as some of them did and were destroyed by the Destroyer. 1 Corinthians 10:10

### I complain when I forget that God is good.

They did not keep God's covenant, but refused to walk according to his law. They forgot his works and the wonders that he had shown them. In the sight of their fathers he performed wonders in the land of Egypt, in the fields of Zoan. He divided the sea and let them pass through it, and made the waters stand like a heap. In the daytime he led them with a cloud, and all the night with a fiery light. He split rocks in the wilderness and gave them drink abundantly as from the deep. He made streams come out of the rock and caused waters to flow down like rivers. Yet they sinned still more against him, rebelling against the Most High in the desert. They tested God in their heart by demanding the food they craved. Psalm 78:10-18

### I am helped when I remember what God has done for me and given me, instead of complaining!

"The LORD has heard your grumbling that you grumble against him—what are we? Your grumbling is not against us but against the LORD." Exodus 16:8b

Oh give thanks to the LORD; call upon his name; make known his deeds among the peoples! Sing to him; sing praises to him; tell of all his wondrous works! Glory in his holy name; let the hearts of those who seek the LORD rejoice! Seek the LORD and his strength; seek his presence continually! Remember the wondrous works that he has done, his miracles and the judgments he uttered. 1 Chronicles 16:8-12

A B C D E F G H I J K L M N O P Q R S T U V W X Y Z

# COMMUNION (THE LORD'S SUPPER)

**Christians take communion to tell others that Jesus has saved them.**

For as often as you eat this bread and drink the cup, you proclaim the Lord's death until he comes. 1 Corinthians 11:26

**Christians take communion to remember Jesus' death on the cross.**

For I received from the Lord what I also delivered to you, that the Lord Jesus on the night when he was betrayed took bread, and when he had given thanks, he broke it, and said, "This is my body which is for you. Do this in remembrance of me." In the same way also he took the cup, after supper, saying, "This cup is the new covenant in my blood. Do this, as often as you drink it, in remembrance of me." 1 Corinthians 11:23-25

**Christians take communion with respect.**

Whoever, therefore, eats the bread or drinks the cup of the Lord in an unworthy manner will be guilty concerning the body and blood of the Lord. Let a person examine himself, then, and so eat of the bread and drink of the cup. 1 Corinthians 11:27-28

# CONFIDENCE

Related topics: Afraid, Shy, Self-Esteem, Faith

**Because God loves me and takes care of me, I can be confident!**

"Have I not commanded you? Be strong and courageous. Do not be frightened, and do not be dismayed, for the LORD your God is with you wherever you go." Joshua 1:9

In the fear of the LORD one has strong confidence, and his children will have a refuge. Proverbs 14:26

The wicked flee when no one pursues, but the righteous are bold as a lion. Proverbs 28:1

Who is like the wise? And who knows the interpretation of a thing? A man's wisdom makes his face shine, and the hardness [boldness] of his face is changed. Ecclesiastes 8:1

I believe that I shall look upon the goodness of the LORD in the land of the living! Wait for the LORD; be strong, and let your heart take courage; wait for the LORD! Psalm 27:13-14

Fear not, for I am with you; be not dismayed, for I am your God; I will strengthen you, I will help you, I will uphold you with my righteous right hand. Isaiah 41:10

**Because Jesus understands my weaknesses, I can be confident that he will help me when I come to him.**
Let us then with confidence draw near to the throne of grace, that we may receive mercy and find grace to help in time of need. Hebrews 4:16.

**I can help others trust God and be confident, too!**
Everyone helps his neighbor and says to his brother, "Be strong!" Isaiah 41:6

**I will have confidence when I am walking with God.**
And now, little children, abide in him, so that when he appears we may have confidence and not shrink from him in shame at his coming. 1 John 2:28

Peter's confidence in Jesus helped him not to be afraid, and to walk on top of water. Matthew 14:25-33

# CONTENTMENT................................

Related topics: Thankfulness, Fairness, Envy/ Jealousy

**Because God is good, I can be content even when I don't get what I want.**

All the days of the afflicted are evil, but the cheerful of heart has a continual feast. Proverbs 15:15

Better is a little with the fear of the LORD than great treasure and trouble with it. Better is a dinner of herbs where love is than a fattened ox and hatred with it. Proverbs 15:16-17

For the LORD God is a sun and shield; the LORD bestows favor and honor. No good thing does he withhold from those who walk uprightly. O LORD of hosts, blessed is the one who trusts in you! Psalm 84:11-12

**Because God is always with me, I can be content even when I don't get what I what.**

Keep your life free from love of money, and be content with what you have, for he has said, "I will never leave you nor forsake you." Hebrews 13:5

**Contentment is difficult to learn, even for adults.**

Not that I am speaking of being in need, for I have learned in whatever situation I am to be content. Philippians 4:11

But if we have food and clothing, with these we will be content. 1 Timothy 6:8

# CREATION

In the beginning, God created the heavens and the earth. Genesis 1:1

By faith we understand that the universe was created by the word of God, so that what is seen was not made out of things that are visible. Hebrews 11:3

**Because God created everything, I know he can do anything.**
'Ah, Lord GOD! It is you who have made the heavens and the earth by your great power and by your outstretched arm! Nothing is too hard for you.' Jeremiah 32:17

**Jesus told us that God made Adam and Eve.**
He answered, "Have you not read that he who created them from the beginning made them male and female..." Matthew 19:4

**God owns everything that he has created, even me!**
Know that the LORD, he is God! It is he who made us, and we are his; we are his people, and the sheep of his pasture. Psalm 100:3

The earth is the LORD's and the fullness thereof, the world and those who dwell therein, for he has founded it upon the seas and established it upon the rivers. Psalm 24:1-2

**Sin ruins God's creation.**
The LORD saw that the wickedness of man was great in the earth, and that every intention of the thoughts of his heart was only evil continually. And the LORD was sorry that he had made man on the earth, and it grieved him to his heart. Genesis 6:5-6

**Jesus came to repair his creation.**

For by grace you have been saved through faith. And this is not your own doing; it is the gift of God, not a result of works, so that no one may boast. For we are his workmanship, created in Christ Jesus for good works, which God prepared beforehand, that we should walk in them.
Ephesians 2:8-10

Therefore, if anyone is in Christ, he is a new creation. The old has passed away; behold, the new has come.
2 Corinthians 5:17

The LORD will fulfill his purpose for me; your steadfast love, O LORD, endures forever. Do not forsake the work of your hands. Psalm 138:8

**God created all things for his own glory and pleasure.**

"Worthy are you, our Lord and God, to receive glory and honor and power, for you created all things, and by your will they existed and were created." Revelation 4:11

For by him all things were created, in heaven and on earth, visible and invisible, whether thrones or dominions or rulers or authorities—all things were created through him and for him. Colossians 1:16

# DEATH

Related topics: Heaven

**When someone I love dies and I am hurting, God promises to stay with me because he is a good shepherd.**

Even though I walk through the valley of the shadow of death, I will fear no evil, for you are with me; your rod and your staff, they comfort me. Psalm 23:4

**God understands and shares my grief.**

The LORD is near to the brokenhearted and saves the crushed in spirit. Psalm 34:18

Now when Mary came to where Jesus was and saw him, she fell at his feet, saying to him, "Lord, if you had been here, my brother would not have died." When Jesus saw her weeping, and the Jews who had come with her also weeping, he was deeply moved in his spirit and greatly troubled. And he said, "Where have you laid him?" They said to him, "Lord, come and see." Jesus wept. So the Jews said, "See how he loved him!" John 11:32-36

Blessed be the God and Father of our Lord Jesus Christ, the Father of mercies and God of all comfort, who comforts us in all our affliction, so that we may be able to comfort those who are in any affliction, with the comfort with which we ourselves are comforted by God. 2 Corinthians 1:3-4

**After a Christian dies, he is with Jesus in heaven.**

I am hard pressed between the two. My desire is to depart and be with Christ, for that is far better. But to remain in the flesh is more necessary on your account. Philippians 1:23-24

Yes, we are of good courage, and we would rather be away from the body and at home with the Lord. So whether we are at home or away, we make it our aim to please him. 2 Corinthians 5:8-9

**The reason we have death is because of sin.**

Therefore, just as sin came into the world through one man, and death through sin, and so death spread to all men because all sinned— Romans 5:12

But each person is tempted when he is lured and enticed by his own desire. Then desire when it has conceived gives birth to sin, and sin when it is fully grown brings forth death. James 1:14-15

# Death of a Pet
Related topics: Death, Pets

## God cares about what happens to even the smallest animals.

Are not five sparrows sold for two pennies? And not one of them is forgotten before God. Luke 12:6

"Six days you shall do your work, but on the seventh day you shall rest; that your ox and your donkey may have rest, and the son of your servant woman, and the alien, may be refreshed." Exodus 23:12

"But ask the beasts, and they will teach you; the birds of the heavens, and they will tell you; or the bushes of the earth, and they will teach you; and the fish of the sea will declare to you. Who among all these does not know that the hand of the LORD has done this? In his hand is the life of every living thing and the breath of all mankind." Job 12:7-10

For every beast of the forest is mine, the cattle on a thousand hills. I know all the birds of the hills, and all that moves in the field is mine. Psalm 50:10-11

## Because God takes care of the birds, I know he will take care of me, too.

Look at the birds of the air: they neither sow nor reap nor gather into barns, and yet your heavenly Father feeds them. Are you not of more value than they? Matthew 6:26

## God cares when I am sad.

Even though I walk through the valley of the shadow of death, I will fear no evil, for you are with me; your rod and your staff, they comfort me. Psalm 23:4

**Although we love our pets very much when they are alive, we do not know what happens to them after they die.**

Who knows whether the spirit of man goes upward and the spirit of the beast goes down into the earth?
Ecclesiastes 3:21

# DISABILITY..............

Related topics: Suffering, Self Esteem

**God made each person with the abilities they need to serve him!**

But Moses said to the LORD, "Oh, my Lord, I am not eloquent, either in the past or since you have spoken to your servant, but I am slow of speech and of tongue." Then the LORD said to him, "Who has made man's mouth? Who makes him mute, or deaf, or seeing, or blind? Is it not I, the LORD? Now therefore go, and I will be with your mouth and teach you what you shall speak." Exodus 4:10-12

I praise you, for I am fearfully and wonderfully made. Wonderful are your works; my soul knows it very well.
Psalm 139:14

**God will fix all the weaknesses and disabilities in heaven!**

He will wipe away every tear from their eyes, and death shall be no more, neither shall there be mourning, nor crying, nor pain anymore, for the former things have passed away." And he who was seated on the throne said, "Behold, I am making all things new." Also he said, "Write this down, for these words are trustworthy and true." Revelation 21:4-5

Then the eyes of the blind shall be opened,and the ears of the deaf unstopped; then shall the lame man leap like a deer, and the tongue of the mute sing for joy. For waters break forth in the wilderness, and streams in the desert; Isaiah 35:5-6

## God shows his power through our weaknesses and disabilities.

As he passed by, he saw a man blind from birth. And his disciples asked him, "Rabbi, who sinned, this man or his parents, that he was born blind?" Jesus answered, "It was not that this man sinned, or his parents, but that the works of God might be displayed in him. John 9:1-3

Three times I pleaded with the Lord about this [Paul's problem], that it should leave me. But he said to me, "My grace is sufficient for you, for my power is made perfect in weakness." Therefore I will boast all the more gladly of my weaknesses, so that the power of Christ may rest upon me. For the sake of Christ, then, I am content with weaknesses, insults, hardships, persecutions, and calamities. For when I am weak, then I am strong. 2 Corinthians 12:8-10

## God gives different abilities to each person, and wants each person to use those abilities for him.

His master said to him, 'Well done, good and faithful servant. You have been faithful over a little; I will set you over much. Enter into the joy of your master.' Matthew 25:23

Read the whole story at Matthew 25:14-29.

## Knowing and loving God is more important than being smart or strong.

His delight is not in the strength of the horse, nor his pleasure in the legs of a man,but the LORD takes pleasure in those who fear him, in those who hope in his steadfast love. Psalm 147:10-11

A B C D E F G H I J K L M N O P Q R S T U V W X Y Z

# DISAPPOINTMENT

Related topics: Contentment, God, Omnipotent

**God is good, and he does not withhold good things from me.**

For the LORD God is a sun and shield; the LORD bestows favor and honor. No good thing does he withhold from those who walk uprightly. Psalm 84:11

**Because God knows the future, I can trust him when I am disappointed.**

Likewise the Spirit helps us in our weakness. For we do not know what to pray for as we ought, but the Spirit himself intercedes for us with groanings too deep for words. Romans 8:28

But Joseph said to them [his brothers], "Do not fear, for am I in the place of God? As for you, you meant evil against me, but God meant it for good, to bring it about that many people should be kept alive, as they are today. Genesis 50:19-20

When Pharaoh let the people go, God did not lead them by way of the land of the Philistines, although that was near. For God said, "Lest the people change their minds when they see war and return to Egypt." But God led the people around by the way of the wilderness toward the Red Sea. And the people of Israel went up out of the land of Egypt equipped for battle. Exodus 13:17-18

**Because God is faithful, I can handle disappointment.**

No temptation has overtaken you that is not common to man. God is faithful, and he will not let you be tempted beyond your ability, but with the temptation he will also provide the way of escape, that you may be able to endure it. 1 Corinthians 10:13

Do not be anxious about anything, but in everything by prayer and supplication with thanksgiving let your requests be made known to God. And the peace of God, which surpasses all understanding, will guard your hearts and your minds in Christ Jesus. Philippians 4:6-7

Trust in the LORD with all your heart, and do not lean on your own understanding. In all your ways acknowledge him, and he will make straight your paths. Proverbs 3:5-6

This God—his way is perfect; the word of the LORD proves true; he is a shield for all those who take refuge in him. Psalm 18:30

Oh, taste and see that the LORD is good! Blessed is the man who takes refuge in him! Psalm 34:8

Though the fig tree should not blossom, nor fruit be on the vines, the produce of the olive fail and the fields yield no food, the flock be cut off from the fold and there be no herd in the stalls, yet I will rejoice in the LORD; I will take joy in the God of my salvation. Habakkuk 3:17-18

> Examples of people who had disappointment: Hagar, Hannah, Esther, Ruth, Paul.
>
> Psalm 34 and Psalm 46 are good Psalms to read when disappointed.

# DIVORCE

See: Parents, Hope, Sadness, Suffering

# ENEMIES

See Bullies, Mean People, Fighting, Forgiveness

# ENVY / JEALOUSY

Related topics: Contentment, Fairness, Thankfulness

**Envy is selfish and destructive.**

A tranquil heart gives life to the flesh, but envy makes the bones rot. Proverbs 14:30

Let us not become conceited, provoking one another, envying one another. Galatians 5:26

For where jealousy and selfish ambition exist, there will be disorder and every vile practice. James 3:16

**God does not want me to be envious of bad people, because their life has a sad ending.**

Truly God is good to Israel, to those who are pure in heart. But as for me, my feet had almost stumbled, my steps had nearly slipped. For I was envious of the arrogant when I saw the prosperity of the wicked... until I went into the sanctuary of God; then I discerned their end. Psalm 73:1-3, 17

**God wants me to learn to trust him with the things or friends I want to have.**

Be still before the LORD and wait patiently for him; fret not yourself over the one who prospers in his way, over the man who carries out evil devices! Psalm 37:7

Be not envious of evil men, nor desire to be with them, for their hearts devise violence, and their lips talk of trouble. Proverbs 24:1-2

**Envy destroys family relationships.**

"And the patriarchs, jealous of Joseph, sold him into Egypt; but God was with him." Acts 7:9 (See also Genesis 37.)

When Rachel saw that she bore Jacob no children, she envied her sister. She said to Jacob, "Give me children, or I shall die!" Jacob's anger was kindled against Rachel, and he said, "Am I in the place of God, who has withheld from you the fruit of the womb?" Genesis 30:1-2

## Envy hurts God's helpers.

And a young man ran and told Moses, "Eldad and Medad are prophesying in the camp." And Joshua the son of Nun, the assistant of Moses from his youth, said, "My lord Moses, stop them." But Moses said to him, "Are you jealous for my sake? Would that all the LORD's people were prophets, that the LORD would put his Spirit on them!" Numbers 11:27-29

> Envy causes people to do bad things. For examples, see Mark 15:9-10 and Acts 17:5.
>
> Miriam and Aaron were envious of Moses. Numbers 12:1-15

A
B
C
D
E
F
G
H
I
J
K
L
M
N
O
P
Q
R
S
T
U
V
W
X
Y
Z

# Evangelism (Telling People about Jesus)

Related topics: Gospel, Salvation, Repentance

**I show others that I follow Jesus when I love other Christians.**

By this all people will know that you are my disciples, if you have love for one another." John 13:35

**I please God when I tell what he has done and is doing in my life.**

Oh give thanks to the LORD; call upon his name; make known his deeds among the peoples! Sing to him, sing praises to him; tell of all his wondrous works! Glory in his holy name; let the hearts of those who seek the LORD rejoice! Seek the LORD and his strength; seek his presence continually! Remember the wondrous works that he has done, his miracles, and the judgments he uttered. Psalm 105:1-5

"Go therefore and make disciples of all nations, baptizing them in the name of the Father and of the Son and of the Holy Spirit, teaching them to observe all that I have commanded you. And behold, I am with you always, to the end of the age." Matthew 28:19-20

**I tell other people about God by living like Jesus.**

Even a child makes himself known by his acts, by whether his conduct is pure and upright. Proverbs 20:11

In the same way, let your light shine before others, so that they may see your good works and give glory to your Father who is in heaven. Matthew 5:16

Do all things without grumbling or questioning [arguing], that you may be blameless and innocent, children of God without blemish in the midst of a crooked and twisted generation, among whom you shine as lights in the world, holding fast to the word of life, so that in the day of Christ I may be proud that I did not run in vain or labor in vain. Philippians 2:14-16

But I say to you, Love your enemies and pray for those who persecute you, so that you may be sons of your Father who is in heaven. For he makes his sun rise on the evil and on the good, and sends rain on the just and on the unjust. For if you love those who love you, what reward do you have? Do not even the tax collectors do the same? And if you greet only your brothers, what more are you doing than others? Do not even the Gentiles do the same? Matthew 5:44-47

Psalm 96 tells God's people to tell others about their wonderful God.

See how God uses children in his plans. Naaman (2 Kings 5:2-15), Rhoda (Acts 12:13-17) The little boy who shared his lunch (John 6:9-14).

# FAIRNESS

Related topics: Anger, Envy, Humility, Contentment

**God is just. He gives each person what is right, even though it may be different.**
Now there are varieties of gifts, but the same Spirit;
1 Corinthians 12:4

For God is not unjust so as to overlook your work and the love that you have shown for his name in serving the saints, as you still do. Hebrews 6:10

Let the nations be glad and sing for joy, for you judge the peoples with equity and guide the nations upon earth. Selah
Psalm 67:4

**Jesus does not want me to fight about fairness. He wants me to remember that the best things are not things I can hold.**
Someone in the crowd said to him, "Teacher, tell my brother to divide the inheritance with me." But he said to him, "Man, who made me a judge or arbitrator over you?" And he said to them, "Take care, and be on your guard against all covetousness, for one's life does not consist in the abundance of his possessions." Luke 12:13-15

But when they measure themselves by one another and compare themselves with one another, they are without understanding. 2 Corinthians 10:12b

**God wants me to look for ways that I can help and please others, before I look for ways to please myself. Jesus set the example for me to follow.**
Let each of you look not only to his own interests, but also to the interests of others. Philippians 2:4

We who are strong have an obligation to bear with the failings of the weak, and not to please ourselves. Let each of us please his neighbor for his good, to build him up. For Christ did not please himself,  Romans 15:1-3a

And they came to Capernaum. And when he was in the house he asked them, "What were you discussing on the way?" But they kept silent, for on the way they had argued with one another about who was the greatest. And he sat down and called the twelve. And he said to them, "If anyone would be first, he must be last of all and servant of all." Mark 9:33-35

**God does not want his children treating each other unfairly and dishonestly.**

Have we not all one Father? Has not one God created us? Why then are we faithless to one another, profaning the covenant of our fathers? Malachi 2:10

A false balance [cheating] is an abomination to the Lord: but a just weight [honesty] is his delight. Proverbs 11:1

He has told you, O man, what is good; and what does the LORD require of you but to do justice, and to love kindness, and to walk humbly with your God? Micah 6:8

See Matthew 20:1-15 for a story about God's justice and differences.

Paul helps the whole church in Corinth learn about fairness and differences in 1 Corinthians 12.

Read about an older brother had problems being too worried about fairness. Luke 15:11-32

# FAITH

Related topic: Trust

**Faith is believing what God says.**

For what does the Scripture say? "Abraham believed God, and it was counted to him as righteousness." Romans 4:3

**God is faithful. I can have faith in him.**

And without faith it is impossible to please him, for whoever would draw near to God must believe that he exists and that he rewards those who seek him.  Hebrews 11:6

For we walk by faith, not by sight. 2 Corinthians 5:7

By faith Sarah herself received power to conceive, even when she was past the age, since she considered him faithful who had promised. Hebrews 11:11

For we hold that one is justified by faith apart from works of the law. Romans 3:28

**Faith comes from God.**

Looking to Jesus, the founder and perfecter of our faith. Hebrews 12:2a

The apostles said to the Lord, "Increase our faith!" Luke 17:5

For by grace you have been saved through faith. And this is not your own doing; it is the gift of God, not a result of works, so that no one may boast. Ephesians 2:8-9

**Faith is remembering what God has done in the past, and believing he will work in the future.**

I will remember the deeds of the LORD; yes, I will remember your wonders of old. I will ponder all your work, and meditate on your mighty deeds. Psalm 77:11-12

Let me hear in the morning of your steadfast love, for in you I trust. Make me know the way I should go, for to you I lift up my soul. Psalm 143: 8

That the next generation might know them [God's teachings], the children yet unborn, and arise and tell them to their children, so that they should set their hope in God and not forget the works of God, but keep his commandments; and that they should not be like their fathers, a stubborn and rebellious generation, a generation whose heart was not steadfast, whose spirit was not faithful to God. Psalm 78:6-8

### The Holy Spirit increases my faith when I listen to the Bible.

So faith comes from hearing, and hearing through the word of Christ. Romans 10:17

### Faith helps me to obey even when I don't understand all the details.

By faith Abraham obeyed when he was called to go out to a place that he was to receive as an inheritance. And he went out, not knowing where he was going. Hebrews 11:8

In all circumstances take up the shield of faith, with which you can extinguish all the flaming darts of the evil one; Ephesians 6:16

And do not seek what you are to eat and what you are to drink, nor be worried. For all the nations of the world seek after these things, and your Father knows that you need them. Instead, seek his kingdom, and these things will be added to you. Luke 12:29-31

Consider the ravens: they neither sow nor reap, they have neither storehouse nor barn, and yet God feeds them. Of how much more value are you than the birds! And which of you by being anxious can add a single hour to his span of life? If then you are not able to do as small a thing as that, why are you anxious about the rest? Luke 12:24-26

Consider the lilies, how they grow: they neither toil nor spin, yet I tell you, even Solomon in all his glory was not arrayed like one of these. But if God so clothes the grass, which is alive in the field today, and tomorrow is thrown into the oven, how much more will he clothe you, O you of little faith! Luke 12:27-28

**Without faith, I am fearful.**
And behold, there arose a great storm on the sea, so that the boat was being swamped by the waves; but he was asleep. And they went and woke him, saying, "Save us, Lord; we are perishing." And he said to them, "Why are you afraid, O you of little faith?" Then he rose and rebuked the winds and the sea, and there was a great calm. And the men marveled, saying, "What sort of man is this, that even winds and sea obey him?" Matthew 8:24-27

> The Roman soldier had great faith because he knew Jesus had the authority to heal his servant, even from far away. Matthew 8:5-10
>
> A woman asked Jesus to help her daughter because she believed he was God, and that he was good. Matthew 15:22-28

# FEAR

See Afraid

# FEAR OF GOD

Related topic: Wisdom

In the fear of the LORD one has strong confidence, and his children will have a refuge. Proverbs 14:26

He gives to the beasts their food, and to the young ravens that cry. His delight is not in the strength of the horse, nor his pleasure in the legs of a man, but the LORD takes pleasure in those who fear him, in those who hope in his steadfast love. Psalm 147:9-11

### God wants me to learn about the fear of God

Come, O children, listen to me; I will teach you the fear of the LORD. Psalm 34:11

### Knowing and loving God's goodness and greatness helps me fear God!

Teach me your way, O LORD, that I may walk in your truth; unite my heart to fear your name. I give thanks to you, O Lord my God, with my whole heart, and I will glorify your name forever. Psalm 86:11-12

If you, O LORD, should mark iniquities, O Lord, who could stand? But with you there is forgiveness, that you may be feared. Psalm 130:3-4

### Knowing God's justice helps me fear God. He rewards my actions, both good and bad.

Then all mankind fears; they tell what God has brought about and ponder what he has done. Psalm 64:9

Do not be deceived: God is not mocked, for whatever one sows, that will he also reap. Galatians 6:7

And by the fear of the LORD one turns away from evil. Proverbs 16:6b

A
B
C
D
E
F
G
H
I
J
K
L
M
N
O
P
Q
R
S
T
U
V
W
X
Y
Z

**God promises that I will learn how to fear God when I search for wisdom!**

The fear of the Lord is the beginning of wisdom!
Proverbs 9:10a

My son, if you receive my words and treasure up my commandments with you, making your ear attentive to wisdom and inclining your heart to understanding; yes, if you call out for insight and raise your voice for understanding, if you seek it like silver and search for it as for hidden treasures, then you will understand the fear of the LORD and find the knowledge of God. Proverbs 2:1-5

The fear of the LORD is hatred of evil. Pride and arrogance and the way of evil and perverted speech I hate.
Proverbs 8:13

**When I have the fear of God, I will not want to run away from Him.**

I will make with them an everlasting covenant, that I will not turn away from doing good to them. And I will put the fear of me in their hearts, that they may not turn from me.
Jeremiah 32:40

Ananias and Sapphira lied to God. When they died because of their sin, many people feared God. Acts 5:1-11

When God protected Daniel in the lion's den, Darius decreed that all people were to tremble and fear before the God of Daniel. Daniel 6, especially verses 26 and 27.

# FIGHTING (STRIFE)

Related topics: Forgiveness, Enemies, Mean People

Behold, how good and pleasant it is when brothers dwell in unity! Psalm 133:1

By insolence comes nothing but strife, but with those who take advice is wisdom. Proverbs 13:10

What causes quarrels and what causes fights among you? Is it not this, that your passions are at war within you? James 4:1

Love one another with brotherly affection. Outdo one another in showing honor. Romans 12:10

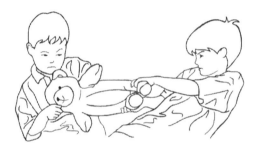

It is an honor for a man to keep aloof from strife, but every fool will be quarreling. Proverbs 20:3

**God wants me to love people even when it is hard.**

But I say to you, Love your enemies and pray for those who persecute you, Matthew 5:44

If possible, so far as it depends on you, live peaceably with all. Romans 12:18

A soft answer turns away wrath, but a harsh word stirs up anger. Proverbs 15:1

A B C D E F G H I J K L M N O P Q R S T U V W X Y Z

**My Heavenly Father is a peacemaker. When I am a peacemaker, I am like him!**

"Blessed are the peacemakers, for they shall be called sons of God." Matthew 5:9

All this is from God, who through Christ reconciled us to himself and gave us the ministry of reconciliation;
2 Corinthians 5:18

Beloved, let us love one another, for love is from God, and whoever loves has been born of God and knows God. Anyone who does not love does not know God, because God is love.
1 John 4:7-8

**When God forgives me, he shows me how to forgive and be kind!**

Let all bitterness and wrath and anger and clamor and slander be put away from you, along with all malice. Be kind to one another, tenderhearted, forgiving one another, as God in Christ forgave you. Ephesians 4:31-32

So then let us pursue what makes for peace and for mutual upbuilding. Romans 14:19

God sent the flood to earth because of violence and fighting: Genesis 6:13. God hates those who love violence: Psalm 11:5.

Jesus told his disciples how to stop fighting: Luke 22:24-27.

# FORGETTING

Related topic: Remember

**I need God's help so I will not forget to obey!**

I have gone astray like a lost sheep; seek your servant, for I do not forget your commandments. Psalm 119:176

I am small and despised, yet I do not forget your precepts. Psalm 119:141

**God wants me to forget about how I have failed in the past, and work on obeying him today.**

Brothers, I do not consider that I have made it my own. But one thing I do: forgetting what lies behind and straining forward to what lies ahead, I press on toward the goal for the prize of the upward call of God in Christ Jesus. Philippians 3:13-14

**Knowing and wanting what pleases God helps me not to forget to do things that please God!**

Do not neglect to do good and to share what you have, for such sacrifices are pleasing to God. Hebrews 13:16

Do not neglect to show hospitality to strangers, for thereby some have entertained angels unawares. Hebrews 13:2

**Doing what the Bible says helps me to remember what the Bible says.**

But be doers of the word, and not hearers only, deceiving yourselves. For if anyone is a hearer of the word and not a doer, he is like a man who looks intently at his natural face in a mirror. For he looks at himself and goes away and at once forgets what he was like. But the one who looks into the perfect law, the law of liberty, and perseveres, being no hearer who forgets but a doer who acts, he will be blessed in his doing. James 1:22-25

My son, do not forget my teaching, but let your heart keep my commandments, for length of days and years of life and peace they will add to you. Proverbs 3:1-2

That the next generation might know them, the children yet unborn, and arise and tell them to their children, so that they should set their hope in God and not forget the works of God, but keep his commandments; and that they should not be like their fathers, a stubborn and rebellious generation, a generation whose heart was not steadfast, whose spirit was not faithful to God. Psalm 78:6-8

### I can remember God's work by singing songs about what he has done for me.

Bless the LORD, O my soul, and all that is within me, bless his holy name! Bless the LORD, O my soul, and forget not all his benefits, who forgives all your iniquity, who heals all your diseases, who redeems your life from the pit, who crowns you with steadfast love and mercy, who satisfies you with good so that your youth is renewed like the eagle's. Psalm 103:1-5

### Sometimes it is wise to forget small offenses against me.

Good sense makes one slow to anger, and it is his glory to overlook an offense. Proverbs 19:11

### God does not forget his children!

"Can a woman forget her nursing child, that she should have no compassion on the son of her womb? Even these may forget, yet I will not forget you. Behold, I have engraved you on the palms of my hands; your walls are continually before me." Isaiah 49:15-16

### Pastors remind us to do right so we don't forget.

Therefore I intend always to remind you of these qualities, though you know them and are established in the truth that you have. 2 Peter 1:12 (See also 2 Timothy 2:14.)

# FORGIVENESS

**Because God is faithful and righteous, he will forgive me when I repent from my sin.**

If we confess our sins, he is faithful and just to forgive us our sins and to cleanse us from all unrighteousness. 1 John 1:9

He does not deal with us according to our sins, nor repay us according to our iniquities. For as high as the heavens are above the earth, so great is his steadfast love toward those who fear him; as far as the east is from the west, so far does he remove our transgressions from us. As a father shows compassion to his children, so the LORD shows compassion to those who fear him. Psalm 103:10-13

**Jesus teaches that I cannot be right with God if I refuse to forgive others.**

"And whenever you stand praying, forgive, if you have anything against anyone, so that your Father also who is in heaven may forgive you your trespasses." Mark 11:25

Be kind to one another, tenderhearted, forgiving one another, as God in Christ forgave you. Ephesians 4:32

**Jesus teaches that part of forgiving others is patience and compassion.**

So the servant fell on his knees, imploring him, 'Have patience with me, and I will pay you everything.' And out of pity for him, the master of that servant released him and forgave him the debt. Matthew 18:26-27

Then Peter came up and said to him, "Lord, how often will my brother sin against me, and I forgive him? As many as seven times?" Jesus said to him, "I do not say to you seven times, but seventy times seven." Matthew 18:21-22

**Jesus wants me to be kind when I have been mistreated.**

But I say to you, Love your enemies and pray for those who persecute you. Matthew 5:44

> Joseph forgave his brothers. Genesis 45:4-8

# FRIENDS

Related topic: Lonely

### God tells me what kind of friends to look for.

Whoever walks with the wise becomes wise, but the companion of fools will suffer harm. Proverbs 13:20

I am a companion of all who fear you, of those who keep your precepts. Psalm 119:63

Make no friendship with a man given to anger, nor go with a wrathful man, lest you learn his ways and entangle yourself in a snare. Proverbs 22:24-25

### God tells me how to be a good friend.

Whoever covers an offense seeks love, but he who repeats a matter separates close friends. Proverbs 17:9

Whoever blesses his neighbor with a loud voice, rising early in the morning, will be counted as cursing. Proverbs 27:14

### True friends help each other do right!

Iron sharpens iron, and one man sharpens another. Proverbs 27:17

Faithful are the wounds of a friend; profuse are the kisses of an enemy. Proverbs 27:6

Come and hear, all you who fear God, and I will tell what he has done for my soul. Psalm 66:16

## True friends ask each other to pray for them.

Therefore, confess your sins to one another and pray for one another, that you may be healed. The prayer of a righteous person has great power as it is working. James 5:16

A friend loves at all times, and a brother is born for adversity. Proverbs 17:17

## Jesus wants to be my friend! He is the best friend to have.

Greater love has no one than this, that someone lay down his life for his friends. You are my friends if you do what I command you. No longer do I call you servants, for the servant does not know what his master is doing; but I have called you friends, for all that I have heard from my Father I have made known to you. John 15:13-15

And the Scripture was fulfilled that says, "Abraham believed God, and it was counted to him as righteousness"—and he was called a friend of God. James 2:23

## When Paul missed his friends, he was reminded to pray for them.

I thank my God in all my remembrance of you, always in every prayer of mine for you all making my prayer with joy... For God is my witness, how I yearn for you all with the affection of Christ Jesus. Philippians 1:3-4, 8

A B C D E F G H I J K L M N O P Q R S T U V W X Y Z

I thank God whom I serve, as did my ancestors, with a clear conscience, as I remember you constantly in my prayers night and day. As I remember your tears, I long to see you, that I may be filled with joy. 2 Timothy 1:3-4

**Sometimes we feel lonely when friends reject us.**
My friends and companions stand aloof from my plague, and my nearest kin stand far off. Psalm 38:11

At my first defense no one came to stand by me, but all deserted me. May it not be charged against them!
2 Timothy 4:16

Examples of friends in the Bible: Jonathan and David; Paul and Onesiphorus 2 Timothy 1:16-18; Ruth and Naomi.

# Fruit of the Spirit

Related topic: Holy Spirit

**The fruit of the spirit is for all Christians: girls and boys, quiet and loud, old and young!**
But the fruit of the Spirit is love, joy, peace, patience, kindness, goodness, faithfulness, gentleness, self-control; against such things there is no law. Galatians 5:22-23

(for the fruit of light is found in all that is good and right and true) Ephesians 5:9

For the moment all discipline seems painful rather than pleasant, but later it yields the peaceful fruit of righteousness to those who have been trained by it. Hebrews 12:11

# Give Up

He gives power to the faint, and to him who has no might he increases strength. Even youths shall faint and be weary, and young men shall fall exhausted; but they who wait for the LORD shall renew their strength; they shall mount up with wings like eagles; they shall run and not be weary; they shall walk and not faint. Isaiah 40:29-31

**I am sometimes tired of doing right, but I know God promises to reward me for not giving up.**
And let us not grow weary of doing good, for in due season we will reap, if we do not give up. Galatians 6:9

For God is not unjust so as to overlook your work and the love that you have shown for his name in serving the saints, as you still do. Hebrews 6:10

**God promises a special blessing if I don't give up after hearing God's Word, and instead obey it!**

But the one who looks into the perfect law, the law of liberty, and perseveres, being no hearer who forgets but a doer who acts, he will be blessed in his doing. James 1:25

But as for you, continue in what you have learned and have firmly believed, knowing from whom you learned it
2 Timothy 3:14

**I can encourage my friends not to give up.**

Whenever Moses held up his hand, Israel prevailed, and whenever he lowered his hand, Amalek prevailed. But Moses' hands grew weary, so they took a stone and put it under him, and he sat on it, while Aaron and Hur held up his hands, one on one side, and the other on the other side. So his hands were steady until the going down of the sun. And Joshua overwhelmed Amalek and his people with the sword. Exodus 17:11-13

**God helps me not give up when I have failed, and I can have courage to start doing right again.**

For the righteous falls seven times and rises again, but the wicked stumble in times of calamity. Proverbs 24:16

**I am encouraged by remembering how Jesus did not give up at the cross.**

Therefore, since we are surrounded by so great a cloud of witnesses, let us also lay aside every weight, and sin which clings so closely, and let us run with endurance the race that is set before us, looking to Jesus, the founder and perfecter of our faith, who for the joy that was set before him endured the cross, despising the shame, and is seated at the right hand of the throne of God. Hebrews 12:1-2

Consider him who endured from sinners such hostility against himself, so that you may not grow weary or faint-hearted. Hebrews 12:3

### God wants me to give up sin!

A desire fulfilled is sweet to the soul, but to turn away from evil is an abomination to fools. Proverbs 13:19

> Elijah was in danger and felt all alone when he wanted to give up. God encouraged him in 1 Kings 19.
>
> Jonah was angry when God forgave people he hated. His anger caused him to want to give up. Jonah 4.

# GIVING

### God wants me to give happily.

Each one must give as he has decided in his heart, not reluctantly or under compulsion, for God loves a cheerful giver. 2 Corinthians 9:7

### God wants me to give to please Him, not to impress others!

"Beware of practicing your righteousness before other people in order to be seen by them, for then you will have no reward from your Father who is in heaven. Thus, when you give to the needy, sound no trumpet before you, as the hypocrites do in the synagogues and in the streets, that they may be praised by others. Truly, I say to you, they have received their reward. But when you give to the needy, do not let your left hand know what your right hand is doing, so that your giving may be in secret. And your Father who sees in secret will reward you." Matthew 6:1-4

A B C D E F G H I J K L M N O P Q R S T U V W X Y Z

**God does not want me to give money if I do not have it.**
For if the readiness is there, it is acceptable according to what a person has, not according to what he does not have. 2 Corinthians 8:12

**I cannot please God by giving without loving.**
If I give away all I have, and if I deliver up my body to be burned, but have not love, I gain nothing. 1 Corinthians 13:3

> The people were so happy to be helping build the tabernacle that Moses had to tell them to stop bringing things when they had enough! Exodus 36:1-7
>
> Jesus loves to use little things in his plans! Proverbs 30:24-28, 1 Corinthians 1:26-28

# GOD
Related topics: Omniscience, Omnipotence, Knowing God

**God is good.**
This God—his way is perfect; the word of the LORD proves true; he is a shield for all those who take refuge in him. Psalm 18:30

I believe that I shall look upon the goodness of the LORD in the land of the living! Wait for the LORD; be strong, and let your heart take courage; wait for the LORD! Psalm 27:13-14

## God is faithful.

Know therefore that the LORD your God is God, the faithful God who keeps covenant and steadfast love with those who love him and keep his commandments, to a thousand generations, Deuteronomy 7:9

I will sing of the steadfast love of the LORD, forever; with my mouth I will make known your faithfulness to all generations. Psalm 89:1

The steadfast love of the LORD never ceases; his mercies never come to an end; they are new every morning; great is your faithfulness. Lamentations 3:22-23

## God is love.

The LORD appeared to him from far away. I have loved you with an everlasting love; therefore I have continued my faithfulness to you. Jeremiah 31:3

"For God so loved the world, that he gave his only Son, that whoever believes in him should not perish but have eternal life." John 3:16

How precious is your steadfast love, O God! The children of mankind take refuge in the shadow of your wings. Psalm 36:7

# GOING TO CHURCH

### God's church is very important to him!

If I delay, you may know how one ought to behave in the household of God, which is the church of the living God, a pillar and buttress of the truth. 1 Timothy 3:15

### God's children like going to church.

I was glad when they said to me, "Let us go to the house of the LORD!" Psalm 122:1

For a day in your courts is better than a thousand elsewhere. I would rather be a doorkeeper in the house of my God than dwell in the tents of wickedness. Psalm 84:10

A
B
C
D
E
F
G
H
I
J
K
L
M
N
O
P
Q
R
S
T
U
V
W
X
Y
Z

Your words were found, and I ate them, and your words became to me a joy and the delight of my heart, for I am called by your name, O LORD, God of hosts. Jeremiah 15:16

### God's children learn God's ways at church.

Assemble the people, men, women, and little ones, and the sojourner within your towns, that they may hear and learn to fear the LORD your God, and be careful to do all the words of this law. Deuteronomy 31:12

For I was envious of the arrogant when I saw the prosperity of the wicked... until I went into the sanctuary of God; then I discerned their end. Psalm 73:3, 17

### God's children help other Christians at church.

And let us consider how to stir up one another to love and good works, not neglecting to meet together, as is the habit of some, but encouraging one another, and all the more as you see the Day drawing near. Hebrews 10:24-25

# GOSPEL

Related topics: Jesus, Salvation, Repentance

### Gospel means "good news." In the Bible, the gospel means the story of Jesus. (See Jesus.)

And the angel said to them, "Fear not, for behold, I bring you good news of great joy that will be for all the people. For unto you is born this day in the city of David a Savior, who is Christ the Lord." Luke 2:10-11

The Spirit of the Lord GOD is upon me, because the LORD has anointed me to bring good news to the poor; he has sent me to bind up the brokenhearted, to proclaim liberty to the captives, and the opening of the prison to those who are bound; Isaiah 61:1 (Jesus said this verse was talking about him! See Luke 4:16-21.)

### The gospel tells me about Jesus' birth, death, and resurrection. (See Salvation)

Now I would remind you, brothers, of the gospel I preached to you… For I delivered to you as of first importance what I also received: that Christ died for our sins in accordance with the Scriptures, that he was buried, that he was raised on the third day in accordance with the Scriptures. 1 Corinthians 15:1a, 3-4

But God, being rich in mercy, because of the great love with which he loved us, even when we were dead in our trespasses, made us alive together with Christ—by grace you have been saved— and raised us up with him and seated us with him in the heavenly places in Christ Jesus, so that in the coming ages he might show the immeasurable riches of his grace in kindness toward us in Christ Jesus. Ephesians 2:4-7 (Verses 8 and 9 can be found in the Salvation topic.)

### The gospel tells me about salvation. (See Salvation)

[Jesus said] "The time is fulfilled, and the kingdom of God is at hand; repent and believe in the gospel." Mark 1:15

For I am not ashamed of the gospel, for it is the power of God for salvation to everyone who believes, to the Jew first and also to the Greek. Romans 1:16

But they have not all obeyed the gospel. For Isaiah says, "Lord, who has believed what he has heard from us?" So faith comes from hearing, and hearing through the word of Christ. Romans 1:16-17

### God wants me to tell people the gospel of Jesus and share my life with them. (See Evangelism)

And he said to them, "Go into all the world and proclaim the gospel to the whole creation." Mark 16:15

So, being affectionately desirous of you, we were ready to share with you not only the gospel of God but also our own selves, because you had become very dear to us. 1 Thessalonians 2:8

A
B
C
D
E
F
G
H
I
J
K
L
M
N
O
P
Q
R
S
T
U
V
W
X
Y
Z

# Happy ....................................................

**Knowing and obeying God and his word will make me happy!**

If you know these things, blessed [happy] are you if you do them. John 13:17

I rejoice at your word like one who finds great spoil. Psalm 119:162

I will sing to the LORD as long as I live; I will sing praise to my God while I have being. May my meditation be pleasing to him, for I rejoice in the LORD. Psalm 104:33-34

Your testimonies are my heritage forever, for they are the joy of my heart. Psalm 119:111

Delight yourself in the LORD, and he will give you the desires of your heart. Psalm 37:4

I delight to do your will, O my God; your law is within my heart. Psalm 40:8

**Helping others makes me happy!**

Whoever despises his neighbor is a sinner, but blessed is he who is generous to the poor. Proverbs 14:21

**Learning to be wise makes me happy!**

Blessed is the one who finds wisdom, and the one who gets understanding. Proverbs 3:13

**Trusting in God makes me happy!**

Whoever gives thought to the word will discover good, and blessed is he who trusts in the LORD. Proverbs 16:20

Oh, taste and see that the LORD is good! Blessed is the man who takes refuge in him! Psalm 34:8

### When God forgives me, I am happy and want to shout for joy!

Blessed is the one whose transgression is forgiven, whose sin is covered. Blessed is the man against whom the LORD counts no iniquity, and in whose spirit there is no deceit. For when I kept silent, my bones wasted away through my groaning all day long... I acknowledged my sin to you, and I did not cover my iniquity; I said, "I will confess my transgressions to the LORD," and you forgave the iniquity of my sin. Selah... Be glad in the LORD, and rejoice, O righteous, and shout for joy, all you upright in heart! Psalm 32:1-3, 5, 11

### Jehoshaphat made God his delight.

The LORD was with Jehoshaphat, because he walked in the earlier ways of his father David. He did not seek the Baals, but sought the God of his father and walked in his commandments, and not according to the practices of Israel. Therefore the LORD established the kingdom in his hand. And all Judah brought tribute to Jehoshaphat, and he had great riches and honor. His heart was courageous in the ways of the LORD. And furthermore, he took the high places and the Asherim out of Judah. 2 Chronicles 17:3-6

### God tells me what makes HIM happy!

His delight is not in the strength of the horse, nor his pleasure in the legs of a man, but the LORD takes pleasure in those who fear him, in those who hope in his steadfast love. Psalm 147:10-11

Lying lips are an abomination to the LORD, but those who act faithfully are his delight. Proverbs 12:22

The sacrifice of the wicked is an abomination to the Lord: but the prayer of the upright is his delight. Proverbs 15:8

Those of crooked [stubbornly disobedient] heart are an abomination to the LORD, but those of blameless ways are his delight. Proverbs 11:20

A B C D E F G H I J K L M N O P Q R S T U V W X Y Z

# HEAVEN

**Nobody will cry in heaven; nobody will be sad in heaven; nobody will die or hurt in heaven!**

"He will wipe away every tear from their eyes, and death shall be no more, neither shall there be mourning, nor crying, nor pain anymore, for the former things have passed away." Revelation 21:4

**God tells his children what heaven is like: heaven doesn't have a sun or moon. Heaven doesn't have a church building! Heaven is a happy, beautiful place.**

And the city has no need of sun or moon to shine on it, for the glory of God gives it light, and its lamp is the Lamb. Revelation 21:23

And I saw no temple in the city, for its temple is the Lord God the Almighty and the Lamb. Revelation 21:22

**God's children will eat food in heaven, including fruit from a tree that has a different kind of fruit each month.**

Then the angel showed me the river of the water of life, bright as crystal, flowing from the throne of God and of the Lamb through the middle of the street of the city; also, on either side of the river, the tree of life with its twelve kinds of fruit, yielding its fruit each month. The leaves of the tree were for the healing of the nations. Revelation 22:1-2

**God promises a special blessing to his children who are excited and looking forward to being in heaven with Jesus.**

Henceforth there is laid up for me the crown of righteousness, which the Lord, the righteous judge, will award to me on that Day, and not only to me but also to all who have loved his appearing. 2 Timothy 4:8

"Let not your hearts be troubled. Believe in God; believe also in me. In my Father's house are many rooms. If it were not so, would I have told you that I go to prepare a place for you? And if I go and prepare a place for you, I will come again and will take you to myself, that where I am you may be also." John 14:1-3

**God's children look forward to heaven, but they also are happy to serve God on earth!**

I am hard pressed between the two. My desire is to depart and be with Christ, for that is far better. But to remain in the flesh is more necessary on your account. Philippians 1:23-24

# HOLY SPIRIT

**The Holy Spirit gives me spiritual life!**

Jesus answered, "Truly, truly, I say to you, unless one is born of water and the Spirit, he cannot enter the kingdom of God. That which is born of the flesh is flesh, and that which is born of the Spirit is spirit. John 3:5-6

**The Holy Spirit comforts me when I am sad.**

And I will ask the Father, and he will give you another Helper, to be with you forever, even the Spirit of truth, whom the world cannot receive, because it neither sees him nor knows him. You know him, for he dwells with you and will be in you. John 14:16-17

**The Holy Spirit helps me learn and understand the Bible.**

"I still have many things to say to you, but you cannot bear them now. When the Spirit of truth comes, he will guide you into all the truth, for he will not speak on his own authority, but whatever he hears he will speak, and he will declare to you the things that are to come." John 16:12-13

Sanctify them in the truth; your word is truth. John 17:17

A
B
C
D
E
F
G
H
I
J
K
L
M
N
O
P
Q
R
S
T
U
V
W
X
Y
Z

And take the helmet of salvation, and the sword of the Spirit, which is the word of God. Ephesians 6:17

## The Holy Spirit prays for me when I cannot think of the words to say!

Likewise the Spirit helps us in our weakness. For we do not know what to pray for as we ought, but the Spirit himself intercedes for us with groanings too deep for words. And he who searches hearts knows what is the mind of the Spirit, because the Spirit intercedes for the saints according to the will of God. Romans 8:26-27

# HOPE

For you, O Lord, are my hope, my trust, O LORD, from my youth. Psalm 71:5

May the God of hope fill you with all joy and peace in believing, so that by the power of the Holy Spirit you may abound in hope. Romans 15:13

## Because God is good and all powerful, I have hope.

Behold, the eye of the LORD is on those who fear him, on those who hope in his steadfast love. Psalm 33:18

Why are you cast down, O my soul, and why are you in turmoil within me? Hope in God; for I shall again praise him, my salvation. Psalm 42:5

For God alone, O my soul, wait in silence, for my hope is from him. He only is my rock and my salvation, my fortress; I shall not be shaken. On God rests my salvation and my glory; my mighty rock, my refuge is God. Trust in him at all times, O people; pour out your heart before him; God is a refuge for us. Selah Psalm 62:5-8

## I am reminded to hope when I read about God in the Bible.

I wait for the LORD, my soul waits, and in his word I hope; Psalm 130:5

Blessed is he whose help is the God of Jacob, whose hope is in the LORD his God. Psalm 146:5

For whatever was written in former days was written for our instruction, that through endurance and through the encouragement of the Scriptures we might have hope. Romans 15:4

**God is happy when I hope and trust in his care for me.**
But the LORD takes pleasure in those who fear him, in those who hope in his steadfast love. Psalm 147:11

But this I call to mind, and therefore I have hope: The steadfast love of the LORD never ceases; his mercies never come to an end; they are new every morning; great is your faithfulness. "The LORD is my portion," says my soul, "therefore I will hope in him." Lamentations 3:21-24

Rejoice in hope, be patient in tribulation, be constant in prayer. Romans 12:12

For to this end we toil and strive, because we have our hope set on the living God, who is the Savior of all people, especially of those who believe. 1 Timothy 4:10

# HORSES

**God uses horses to teach me what he is like.**
The horse is made ready for the day of battle, but the victory belongs to the LORD.
Proverbs 21:31

Some trust in chariots and some in horses, but we trust in the name of the LORD our God. Psalm 20:7

I will instruct you and teach you in the way you should go; I will counsel you with my eye upon you. Be not like a horse or a mule, without understanding, which must be curbed with bit and bridle, or it will not stay near you. Psalm 32:8-9

Woe to those who go down to Egypt for help and rely on horses, who trust in chariots because they are many and in horsemen because they are very strong, but do not look to the Holy One of Israel or consult the LORD! Isaiah 31:1

His delight is not in the strength of the horse, nor his pleasure in the legs of a man, but the LORD takes pleasure in those who fear him, in those who hope in his steadfast love.
Psalm 147:10-11

"Do you give the horse his might?
Do you clothe his neck with a mane?
Do you make him leap like the locust?
His majestic snorting is terrifying.
He paws in the valley and exults in his strength;
he goes out to meet the weapons.
He laughs at fear and is not dismayed;
he does not turn back from the sword.
Upon him rattle the quiver,
the flashing spear, and the javelin."
Job 39:19-23

The king is not saved by his great army; a warrior is not delivered by his great strength. The war horse is a false hope for salvation, and by its great might it cannot rescue. Behold, the eye of the LORD is on those who fear him, on those who hope in his steadfast love. Psalm 33:16-18

Then I saw heaven opened, and behold, a white horse! The one sitting on it is called Faithful and True, and in righteousness he judges and makes war. His eyes are like a flame of fire, and on his head are many diadems, and he has a name written that no one knows but himself. Revelation 19:11-12

# Humility

Related topics: Pride, Fair, Anger

He has told you, O man, what is good; and what does the LORD require of you but to do justice, and to love kindness, and to walk humbly with your God? Micah 6:8

Likewise, you who are younger, be subject to the elders. Clothe yourselves, all of you, with humility toward one another, for "God opposes the proud but gives grace to the humble." 1 Peter 5:5

### A humble child will not insist on his own way, or become angry when life doesn't seem fair. When he learns to be meek, he will have peace!

Be still before the LORD and wait patiently for him; fret not yourself over the one who prospers in his way, over the man who carries out evil devices! Refrain from anger, and forsake wrath! Fret not yourself; it tends only to evil... But the meek shall inherit the land and delight themselves in abundant peace. Psalm 37: 7-8, 11

### Children learn to be humble when they give others the best choice.

Do nothing from rivalry or conceit, but in humility count others more significant than yourselves. Let each of you look not only to his own interests, but also to the interests of others. Philippians 2:3-4

### God wants his children to be humble like Jesus.

Have this mind among yourselves, which is yours in Christ Jesus, who, though he was in the form of God, did not count equality with God a thing to be grasped, but made himself nothing, taking the form of a servant, being born in the like-ness of men. And being found in human form, he humbled himself by becoming obedient to the point of death, even death on a cross. Philippians 2:5-8

Whoever humbles himself like this child is the greatest in the kingdom of heaven. Matthew 18:4

> Moses was the meekest man on the earth (Numbers 12:3). He was more concerned about others and God's glory than about his own power and success. Numbers 14:11-20

# JESUS

Related topics: God, Holy Spirit

**Jesus came to earth so that I could know God, love him, and be his friend!**

And we know that the Son of God has come and has given us understanding, so that we may know him who is true; and we are in him who is true, in his Son Jesus Christ. He is the true God and eternal life. 1 John 5:20

For to us a child is born, to us a son is given; and the government shall be upon his shoulder,and his name shall be called Wonderful Counselor, Mighty God, Everlasting Father, Prince of Peace. Isaiah 9:6

"This is my commandment, that you love one another as I have loved you. Greater love has no one than this, that someone lay down his life for his friends. You are my friends if you do what I command you." John 15:12-14

Peace I leave with you; my peace I give to you. Not as the world gives do I give to you. Let not your hearts be troubled, neither let them be afraid. John 14:27

## Jesus is the only way to make peace with God.

Jesus said to him, "I am the way, and the truth, and the life. No one comes to the Father except through me." John 14:6

For while we were still weak, at the right time Christ died for the ungodly. For one will scarcely die for a righteous person—though perhaps for a good person one would dare even to die— but God shows his love for us in that while we were still sinners, Christ died for us. Since, therefore, we have now been justified by his blood, much more shall we be saved by him from the wrath of God. Romans 5:6-9

## When Jesus said he was God, some Jews who did not like his words tried to kill him.

[Jesus said:] "I and the Father are one." The Jews picked up stones again to stone him. Jesus answered them, "I have shown you many good works from the Father; for which of them are you going to stone me?" The Jews answered him, "It is not for a good work that we are going to stone you but for blasphemy, because you, being a man, make yourself God." John 10:31-33

This was why the Jews were seeking all the more to kill him, because not only was he breaking the Sabbath, but he was even calling God his own Father, making himself equal with God. John 5:18

Jesus said to them, "Truly, truly, I say to you, before Abraham was, I am." So they picked up stones to throw at him, but Jesus hid himself and went out of the temple. John 8:58-59 (Compare with Exodus 3:14: "I AM.")

## The Bible also shows that Jesus is God when Jesus does things that only God can do.

And when Jesus saw their faith, he said to the paralytic, "Son, your sins are forgiven." Now some of the scribes were sitting there, questioning in their hearts, "Why does this man speak like that? He is blaspheming! Who can forgive sins but God alone?" Mark 2:5-7 (Compare with Isaiah 55:6-7 and Psalm 32:1-2.)

A
B
C
D
E
F
G
H
I
J
K
L
M
N
O
P
Q
R
S
T
U
V
W
X
Y
Z

All things were made through him, and without him was not any thing made that was made. John 1:3 (Also see the story of Jesus creating fish and bread in Mark 6:38-44. Compare with Isaiah 40:28.)

And Jesus answered them, "Go and tell John what you hear and see: the blind receive their sight and the lame walk, lepers are cleansed and the deaf hear, and the dead are raised up, and the poor have good news preached to them. Matthew 11:4-5 (Compare with Isaiah 35:4-8.)

Jesus' birth (Matthew 1:18–2:23 and Luke 1:26–2:22)

When Jesus was a boy (Luke 2:40-52)

Jesus talking about children (Matthew 18:1-6, 10; 19:13-24)

Jesus prayed for me! (All of John 17, especially verse 20)

Jesus' death, burial, and resurrection (Matthew 26:47–28:20; Mark 14:43–16:20; Luke 22:47–24:53; John 18-21)

# KINDNESS

Related topic: Love

**One way I can be kind is to forgive others for Jesus' sake, the same way God forgave me!**
Be kind to one another, tenderhearted, forgiving one another, as God in Christ forgave you. Ephesians 4:32

**Another way I can be kind is to be patient, and learn to love others.**

Love is patient and kind; love does not envy or boast; it is not arrogant or rude. It does not insist on its own way; it is not irritable or resentful; 1 Corinthians 13:4-5

But if anyone has the world's goods and sees his brother in need, yet closes his heart against him, how does God's love abide in him? Little children, let us not love in word or talk but in deed and in truth. 1 John 3:17-18

**When I am kind to younger children, or people who seem unimportant, Jesus tells me it's like I'm being kind to HIM!**

Then the righteous will answer him, saying, 'Lord, when did we see you hungry and feed you, or thirsty and give you drink? And when did we see you a stranger and welcome you, or naked and clothe you? And when did we see you sick or in prison and visit you?' And the King will answer them, 'Truly, I say to you, as you did it to one of the least of these my brothers, you did it to me.' Matthew 25:37-40

**God wants me to be kind to my friends and enemies even when they are not being kind back.**

But love your enemies, and do good, and lend, expecting nothing in return, and your reward will be great, and you will be sons of the Most High, for he is kind to the ungrateful and the evil. Luke 6:35

**I can be kind by encouraging my friends who are sad.**

Anxiety in a man's heart weighs him down, but a good word makes him glad. Proverbs 12:25

A B C D E F G H I J K L M N O P Q R S T U V W X Y Z

**God wants me to enjoy thinking ahead and planning ways to be kind.**

Do they not go astray who devise evil? Those who devise good meet steadfast love and faithfulness. Proverbs 14:22

So then, as we have opportunity, let us do good to everyone, and especially to those who are of the household of faith. Galatians 6:10

# KNOWING GOD

**God wants me to try to know him, to look for him.**

But seek first the kingdom of God and his righteousness, and all these things will be added to you. Matthew 6:33

You will seek me and find me, when you seek me with all your heart. Jeremiah 29:13

And those who know your name put their trust in you, for you, O LORD, have not forsaken those who seek you. Psalm 9:10

Draw near to God, and he will draw near to you. Cleanse your hands, you sinners, and purify your hearts, you double-minded. James 4:8

But may all who seek you rejoice and be glad in you; may those who love your salvation say continually, "Great is the LORD!" Psalm 40:16

**God gives me the desire to know him.**

O God, you are my God; earnestly I seek you; my soul thirsts for you; my flesh faints for you, as in a dry and weary land where there is no water. So I have looked upon you in the sanctuary, beholding your power and glory. Because your steadfast love is better than life, my lips will praise you. Psalm 63:1-3

My soul longs, yes, faints for the courts of the LORD; my heart and flesh sing for joy to the living God. Psalm 84:2

As a deer pants for flowing streams, so pants my soul for you, O God. My soul thirsts for God, for the living God. When shall I come and appear before God? My tears have been my food day and night, while they say to me all the day long, "Where is your God?" These things I remember, as I pour out my soul: how I would go with the throng and lead them in procession to the house of God with glad shouts and songs of praise, a multitude keeping festival. Psalm 42:1-4

## God is delighted when I want to know him.

But grow in the grace and knowledge of our Lord and Savior Jesus Christ. To him be the glory both now and to the day of eternity. Amen. 2 Peter 3:18

Thus says the LORD: "Let not the wise man boast in his wisdom, let not the mighty man boast in his might, let not the rich man boast in his riches, but let him who boasts boast in this, that he understands and knows me, that I am the LORD who practices steadfast love, justice, and righteousness in the earth. For in these things I delight, declares the LORD." Jeremiah 9:23-24

> Isaiah 40 is a whole chapter about our wonderful God.
>
> King David wrote Psalms that show what it looks like to know God.
>
> Paul told the church at Philippi that one of his biggest goals was to know God better. Philippians 3:10

# LAZY

See Work

# LEARNING PROBLEMS
See Disability

# LISTENING

**When Jesus was a boy, he listened and asked questions.**
After three days they found him [Jesus] in the temple, sitting among the teachers, listening to them and asking them questions.  Luke 2:46

**God's children learn to listen to and follow Jesus.**
My sheep hear my voice, and I know them, and they follow me. John 10:27

**A foolish child is more interested in his own opinions than listening.**
A fool takes no pleasure in understanding, but only in expressing his opinion. Proverbs 18:2

If one gives an answer before he hears, it is his folly and shame. Proverbs 18:13

**Listening is one way I can learn to control my anger.**
Know this, my beloved brothers: let every person be quick to hear, slow to speak, slow to anger; James 1:19

**Listening to truth will help me to become wise.**
Listen to advice and accept instruction, that you may gain wisdom in the future. Proverbs 19:20

"And now, O sons, listen to me: blessed are those who keep my ways. Hear instruction and be wise, and do not neglect it. Blessed is the one who listens to me, watching daily at my gates, waiting beside my doors." Proverbs 8:32-34

The way of a fool is right in his own eyes, but a wise man listens to advice. Proverbs 12:15

Read a good example of Samuel, who listened well when he was a child, in 1 Samuel 3.

Mary listened with a believing heart when Gabriel told her she would give birth to Jesus. She wrote a poem about it. Luke 1:34-38, and Luke 1:46-55

Zacharias listened with an unbelieving heart when Gabriel told him that his wife would give birth. Luke 1:18-20

A B C D E F G H I J K L M N O P Q R S T U V W X Y Z

# LONELY

Related topic: Friends

## God is my helper and friend when I am lonely.

For he has said, "I will never leave you nor forsake you." So we can confidently say, "The Lord is my helper; I will not fear; what can man do to me?" Hebrews 13:5b-6

Look to the right and see: there is none who takes notice of me; no refuge remains to me; no one cares for my soul. I cry to you, O LORD; I say, "You are my refuge, my portion in the land of the living." Psalm 142:4-5

Save, O LORD, for the godly one is gone; for the faithful have vanished from among the children of man. Everyone utters lies to his neighbor; with flattering lips and a double heart they speak. Psalm 12:1-2

## King David wrote poems of his prayers when he was lonely.

Hear my prayer, O LORD; let my cry come to you! Do not hide your face from me in the day of my distress! Incline your ear to me; answer me speedily in the day when I call! For my days pass away like smoke, and my bones burn like a furnace. My heart is struck down like grass and has withered; I forget to eat my bread. Because of my loud groaning my bones cling to my flesh. I am like a desert owl of the wilderness, like an owl of the waste places; I lie awake; I am like a lonely sparrow on the housetop. Psalm 102:1-7

## Jesus wants to be my friend.

Greater love has no one than this, that someone lay down his life for his friends. You are my friends if you do what I command you. No longer do I call you servants, for the servant does not know what his master is doing; but I have called you friends, for all that I have heard from my Father I have made known to you. John 15:13-15

**God showed me how to find someone who needs a friend.**

Greater love has no one than this, that someone lay down his life for his friends. John 15:13

**When I feel alone, God wants me to come close to him and ask him for help.**

Whom have I in heaven but you? And there is nothing on earth that I desire besides you. My flesh and my heart may fail, but God is the strength of my heart and my portion forever... But for me it is good to be near God; I have made the Lord GOD my refuge, that I may tell of all your works. Psalm 73:25-26, 28

**God will always supply my needs, even though there may be times when I do not have a close friend.**

Then the LORD God said, "It is not good that the man should be alone; I will make him a helper fit for him." Genesis 2:18

And my God will supply every need of yours according to his riches in glory in Christ Jesus. Philippians 4:19

For the LORD God is a sun and shield; the LORD bestows favor and honor. No good thing does he withhold from those who walk uprightly. O LORD of hosts, blessed is the one who trusts in you! Psalm 84:11-12

**Being lonely reminds me that I live for God, and he never forgets my work for him!**

Therefore, my beloved brothers, be steadfast, immovable, always abounding in the work of the Lord, knowing that in the Lord your labor is not in vain. 1 Corinthians 15:58

**I am never truly alone.**

If I take the wings of the morning and dwell in the uttermost parts of the sea, even there your hand shall lead me, and your right hand shall hold me. Psalm 139:9-10

A B C D E F G H I J K L M N O P Q R S T U V W X Y Z

# LOVE

Related topic: God

### God's love sets the example for me to follow.

Beloved, let us love one another, for love is from God, and whoever loves has been born of God and knows God. Anyone who does not love does not know God, because God is love. 1 John 4:7-8

Hereby perceive we the love of God, because he laid down his life for us: and we ought to lay down our lives for the brethren. 1 John 3:16

Beloved, if God so loved us, we also ought to love one another. 1 John 4:11

### God wants me to learn how to love him!

Be very careful, therefore, to love the LORD your God. Joshua 23:11

We love because he first loved us. 1 John 4:19

"And now, Israel, what does the LORD your God require of you, but to fear the LORD your God, to walk in all his ways, to love him, to serve the LORD your God with all your heart and with all your soul." Deuteronomy 10:12

### Love is not just a feeling or something I say; love is something I DO!

Little children, let us not love in word or talk but in deed and in truth. 1 John 3:18

### I can love others by overlooking faults.

A friend loves at all times, and a brother is born for adversity. Proverbs 17:17

Hatred stirs up strife, but love covers all offenses. Proverbs 10:12

Above all, keep loving one another earnestly, since love covers a multitude of sins. 1 Peter 4:8

**I can love by choosing what is best for others.**

Love does no wrong to a neighbor; therefore love is the fulfilling of the law. Romans 13:10

Let love be genuine. Abhor what is evil; hold fast to what is good. Love one another with brotherly affection. Outdo one another in showing honor. Do not be slothful in zeal, be fervent in spirit, serve the Lord. Rejoice in hope, be patient in tribulation, be constant in prayer. Contribute to the needs of the saints and seek to show hospitality. Romans 12:9-13

> The whole chapter of 1 Corinthians 13 is about love.

| | |
|---|---|
| Love is patient. | See Patient |
| Love is kind. | See Kindness |
| Love does not envy. | See Envy/ Jealousy |
| Love does not boast. | See Humility and Pride |
| Love is not arrogant or rude. | See Modest |
| Love does not insist on its own way. | See Selfishness |
| Love is not irritable. | See Anger |
| Love does not rejoice at wrong-doing. | See Hope |
| Love rejoices in truth. | See Truth |

A
B
C
D
E
F
G
H
I
J
K
L
M
N
O
P
Q
R
S
T
U
V
W
X
Y
Z

# LYING ..............

Related topic: Truth Telling

**God hates lying.**

Lying lips are an abomination to the LORD, but those who act faithfully are his delight. Proverbs 12:22

**King David prayed that people would stop lying.**

Let the lying lips be mute, which speak insolently against the righteous in pride and contempt. Psalm 31:18

**I want God to help me love truth and hate lying.**

I hate and abhor falsehood, but I love your law. Psalm 119:163

Let not steadfast love and faithfulness forsake you; bind them around your neck; write them on the tablet of your heart. Proverbs 3:3

Therefore, having put away falsehood, let each one of you speak the truth with his neighbor, for we are members one of another. Ephesians 4:25

Keep your tongue from evil and your lips from speaking deceit. Psalm 34:13

> Achan stole, and then he lied about what he had done. Joshua 7:10-26

# Mean People

Related topics: Enemies, Fighting, Forgiveness

## When I am mean

See that no one repays anyone evil for evil, but always seek to do good to one another and to everyone. 1 Thessalonians 5:15

## When others are mean

Do not rejoice when your enemy falls, and let not your heart be glad when he stumbles, lest the LORD see it and be displeased, and turn away his anger from him. Proverbs 24:17-18

Fret not yourself because of evildoers, and be not envious of the wicked, for the evil man has no future; the lamp of the wicked will be put out. Proverbs 24:19-20

If your enemy is hungry, give him bread to eat, and if he is thirsty, give him water to drink, for you will heap burning coals on his head, and the LORD will reward you.
Proverbs 25:21-22

## God will avenge wrong things in his time.

Beloved, never avenge yourselves, but leave it to the wrath of God, for it is written, "Vengeance is mine, I will repay, says the Lord." To the contrary, "if your enemy is hungry, feed him; if he is thirsty, give him something to drink; for by so doing you will heap burning coals on his head." Do not be overcome by evil, but overcome evil with good.
Romans 12:19-21

## God wants me to stand up to bullies for others who cannot defend themselves.

Learn to do good; seek justice, correct oppression; bring justice to the fatherless, plead the widow's cause. Isaiah 1:17

A B C D E F G H I J K L M N O P Q R S T U V W X Y Z

**God wants me to help those having a hard time.**
And we urge you, brothers, admonish the idle, encourage the fainthearted, help the weak, be patient with them all. 1 Thessalonians 5:14

King David wrote songs when he was troubled with people. See Psalms 35, 56, 57, and 61.

Paul was a mean person until God changed his heart. Read about it starting in Acts 9.

# Modesty .........................................

Related topic: Humility

**Modesty starts with humble and pure thoughts.**
Keep your heart with all vigilance, for from it flow the springs of life. Proverbs 4:23

Do not let your adorning be external—the braiding of hair and the putting on of gold jewelry, or the clothing you wear— but let your adorning be the hidden person of the heart with the imperishable beauty of a gentle and quiet spirit, which in God's sight is very precious. 1 Peter 3:3-4

Or do you not know that your body is a temple of the Holy Spirit within you, whom you have from God? You are not your own, for you were bought with a price. So glorify God in your body. 1 Corinthians 6:19-20

**Modesty results in actions, words, and even clothing chosen to please God, and build up others.**
He has told you, O man, what is good; and what does the LORD require of you but to do justice, and to love kindness, and to walk humbly [modestly] with your God? Micah 6:8

So, whether you eat or drink, or whatever you do, do all to the glory of God. 1 Corinthians 10:31

So then let us pursue what makes for peace and for mutual upbuilding. Romans 14:19

### God want me to dress and act in a way that doesn't show off.

Likewise also that women should adorn themselves in respectable apparel, with modesty and self-control, not with braided hair and gold or pearls or costly attire, but with what is proper for women who profess godliness—with good works.  1 Timothy 2:9-10

Thus says the LORD: "Let not the wise man boast in his wisdom, let not the mighty man boast in his might, let not the rich man boast in his riches, but let him who boasts boast in this, that he understands and knows me, that I am the LORD who practices steadfast love, justice, and righteousness in the earth. For in these things I delight, declares the LORD." Jeremiah 9:23-24

A
B
C
D
E
F
G
H
I
J
K
L
M
N
O
P
Q
R
S
T
U
V
W
X
Y
Z

# MONEY

Related topics: Giving, Contentment

Do not toil to acquire wealth; be discerning enough to desist. Proverbs 23:4

Now there is great gain in godliness with contentment, 1 Timothy 6:6

[Wisdom] is more precious than jewels, and nothing you desire can compare with her. Proverbs 3:15

### God wants me to use money to help others.

As for the rich in this present age, charge them not to be haughty, nor to set their hopes on the uncertainty of riches, but on God, who richly provides us with everything to enjoy. 1 Timothy 6:17

They are to do good, to be rich in good works, to be generous and ready to share. 1 Timothy 6:18

Whoever trusts in his riches will fall, but the righteous will flourish like a green leaf. Proverbs 11:28

### Having a poor, happy home is better than a rich, fighting home.

Better is a little with the fear of the LORD than great treasure and trouble with it. Better is a dinner of herbs where love is than a fattened ox and hatred with it. Proverbs 15:16-17

**The most important things in my life cannot be bought with money.**
And he [Jesus] said to them, "Take care, and be on your guard against all covetousness, for one's life does not consist in the abundance of his possessions." Luke 12:15

# OBEDIENCE

Children, obey your parents in the Lord, for this is right. Ephesians 6:1

And the people said to Joshua, "The LORD our God we will serve, and his voice we will obey." Joshua 24:24

When I think on my ways, I turn my feet to your testimonies; I hasten and do not delay to keep your commandments. Psalm 119:59-60

**Jesus was a good example as a boy. He obeyed his parents, even they didn't understand him!**
And they did not understand the saying that he spoke to them. And he went down with them and came to Nazareth and was submissive to them. And his mother treasured up all these things in her heart. Luke 2:50-51

**God wants me to obey other authorities, too.**
Remind them to be submissive to rulers and authorities, to be obedient, to be ready for every good work, to speak evil of no one, to avoid quarreling, to be gentle, and to show perfect courtesy toward all people. Titus 3:1-2

Obey your leaders and submit to them, for they are keeping watch over your souls, as those who will have to give an account. Let them do this with joy and not with groaning, for that would be of no advantage to you. Hebrews 13:17

# OMNIPOTENT

**God can do anything he wants to do.**

"For nothing will be impossible with God." Luke 1:37

'Ah, Lord GOD! It is you who have made the heavens and the earth by your great power and by your outstretched arm! Nothing is too hard for you.' Jeremiah 32:17

He heals the brokenhearted and binds up their wounds. He determines the number of the stars; he gives to all of them their names. Great is our Lord, and abundant in power; his understanding is beyond measure. Psalm 147:3-5

**God's power gives me hope.**

May the God of hope fill you with all joy and peace in believing, so that by the power of the Holy Spirit you may abound in hope. Romans 15:13

# OMNIPRESENT

**God is everywhere present at all times.**

The eyes of the LORD are in every place, keeping watch on the evil and the good. Proverbs 15:3

Where shall I go from your Spirit? Or where shall I flee from your presence? If I ascend to heaven, you are there! If I make my bed in Sheol, you are there! If I take the wings of the morning and dwell in the uttermost parts of the sea, even there your hand shall lead me, and your right hand shall hold me. Psalm 139:7-10

"Am I a God at hand, declares the LORD, and not a God far away? Can a man hide himself in secret places so that I cannot see him? declares the LORD. Do I not fill heaven and earth? declares the LORD." Jeremiah 23:23-24

"I am the Alpha and the Omega," says the Lord God, "who is and who was and who is to come, the Almighty." Revelation 1:8

# OMNISCIENCE

### God knows everything about me.

O LORD, you have searched me and known me! You know when I sit down and when I rise up; you discern my thoughts from afar. You search out my path and my lying down and are acquainted with all my ways. Even before a word is on my tongue, behold, O LORD, you know it altogether. You hem me in, behind and before, and lay your hand upon me. Psalm 139:1-5

### God knows when I am disobeying.

But if you will not do so, behold, you have sinned against the LORD, and be sure your sin will find you out. Numbers 32:23

### God knows when I do right.

For the LORD knows the way of the righteous, but the way of the wicked will perish. Psalm 1:6

"For the eyes of the Lord are on the righteous, and his ears are open to their prayer. But the face of the Lord is against those who do evil." 1 Peter 3:12

Oh, the depth of the riches and wisdom and knowledge of God! How unsearchable are his judgments and how inscrutable his ways! "For who has known the mind of the Lord, or who has been his counselor? Or who has given a gift to him that he might be repaid? For from him and through him and to him are all things. To him be glory forever. Amen." Romans 11:33-36

A
B
C
D
E
F
G
H
I
J
K
L
M
N
O
P
Q
R
S
T
U
V
W
X
Y
Z

# PARENTS

**Godly parents are thrilled when their children learn to be wise.**

The father of the righteous will greatly rejoice; he who fathers a wise son will be glad in him. Let your father and mother be glad; let her who bore you rejoice. Proverbs 23:24-25

I have no greater joy than to hear that my children are walking in the truth. 3 John 1:4

Fathers, do not provoke your children to anger, but bring them up in the discipline and instruction of the Lord. Ephesians 6:4

**God wants parents to teach their children to love God's ways, grow up, and teach THEIR children to love God's ways!**

We will not hide them from their children, but tell to the coming generation the glorious deeds of the LORD, and his might, and the wonders that he has done. He established a testimony in Jacob and appointed a law in Israel, which he commanded our fathers to teach to their children. Psalm 78:4-5

**When my parents do not follow Christ, God will help me do right.**

"Can a woman forget her nursing child, that she should have no compassion on the son of her womb? Even these may forget, yet I will not forget you." Isaiah 49:15

For my father and my mother have forsaken me, but the LORD will take me in. Psalm 27:10

That the next generation might know them [God's teachings], the children yet unborn, and arise and tell them to their children, so that they should set their hope in God and not forget the works of God, but keep his commandments; and that they should not be like their fathers, a stubborn and rebellious generation, a generation whose heart was not steadfast, whose spirit was not faithful to God. Psalm 78:6-8

> God uses children who have bad parents and good parents. King Josiah had an ungodly father and grandfather, but he chose to follow God! 2 Kings 22:2, and 22:19
>
> Timothy had a godly mother and grandmother who taught him the Bible when he was young. 2 Timothy 1:5; 3:15

# PATIENCE

Related topics: Anger, Longsuffering

### God is patient.

But you, O Lord, are a God merciful and gracious, slow to anger and abounding in steadfast love and faithfulness. Psalm 86:15

### Because God is patient, I can be patient.

Be still before the LORD and wait patiently for him; Psalm 37:7a

May the God of endurance and encouragement grant you to live in such harmony with one another, in accord with Christ Jesus. Romans 15:5

A B C D E F G H I J K L M N O P Q R S T U V W X Y Z

Pursue righteousness, godliness, faith, love, steadfastness, gentleness. 1 Timothy 6:11b

I therefore, a prisoner for the Lord, urge you to walk in a manner worthy of the calling to which you have been called, with all humility and gentleness, with patience, bearing with one another in love. Ephesians 4:1-2

Be not quick in your spirit to become angry, for anger lodges in the bosom of fools. Ecclesiastes 7:9

**I learn to be patient when I study and follow Christ's example of patience.**
Looking to Jesus, the founder and perfecter of our faith, who for the joy that was set before him endured the cross, despising the shame, and is seated at the right hand of the throne of God. Consider him who endured from sinners such hostility against himself, so that you may not grow weary or fainthearted. Hebrews 12:2-3

**Because God is a righteous judge, I can give my case to God and believe that he will judge those who have wronged me and treated me badly.**
For to this you have been called, because Christ also suffered for you, leaving you an example, so that you might follow in his steps. He committed no sin, neither was deceit found in his mouth. When he was reviled, he did not revile in return; when he suffered, he did not threaten, but continued entrusting himself to him who judges justly. 1 Peter 2:21-23

# Peace

**All peace comes from God!**

For to us a child is born, to us a son is given; and the government shall be upon his shoulder, and his name shall be called Wonderful Counselor, Mighty God, Everlasting Father, Prince of Peace. Isaiah 9:6

May grace and peace be multiplied to you in the knowledge of God and of Jesus our Lord. 2 Peter 1:2

But the fruit of the Spirit is love, joy, peace... Galatians 5:22a

**God first gives me peace when I become a Christian.**

Therefore, since we have been justified by faith, we have peace with God through our Lord Jesus Christ. Romans 5:1

May the God of hope fill you with all joy and peace in believing, so that by the power of the Holy Spirit you may abound in hope. Romans 15:13

**God gives peace to me as I learn to love the Bible.**

Great peace have those who love your law; nothing can make them stumble. Psalm 119:165

**God gives peace to me as I think about how much God loves me and takes care of me!**

You keep him in perfect peace whose mind is stayed on you, because he trusts in you. Isaiah 26:3

Peace I leave with you; my peace I give to you. Not as the world gives do I give to you. Let not your hearts be troubled, neither let them be afraid. John 14:27

A
B
C
D
E
F
G
H
I
J
K
L
M
N
O
P
Q
R
S
T
U
V
W
X
Y
Z

**God gives peace to me as I learn to pray.**

Do not be anxious about anything, but in everything by prayer and supplication with thanksgiving let your requests be made known to God. And the peace of God, which surpasses all understanding, will guard your hearts and your minds in Christ Jesus. Philippians 4:6-7

**God gives peace to me as I learn to think about good things.**

Finally, brothers, whatever is true, whatever is honorable, whatever is just, whatever is pure, whatever is lovely, whatever is commendable, if there is any excellence, if there is anything worthy of praise, think about these things. What you have learned and received and heard and seen in me—practice these things, and the God of peace will be with you. Philippians 4:8-9

# PERSEVERANCE

See Give Up

# PETS

Whoever is righteous has regard for the life of his beast, but the mercy of the wicked is cruel. Proverbs 12:10

For the Scripture says, "You shall not muzzle an ox when it treads out the grain," and, "The laborer deserves his wages." 1 Timothy 5:18

> The Prophet Nathan told David a story about a pet lamb in order to teach him an important lesson. 2 Samuel 12:1-6

# Prayer
...............................................................

## God loves to hear Christians pray to him.

The sacrifice of the wicked is an abomination to the LORD, but the prayer of the upright is acceptable to him. Proverbs 15:8

The eyes of the LORD are toward the righteous and his ears toward their cry. Psalm 34:15

"Ask, and it will be given to you; seek, and you will find; knock, and it will be opened to you. For everyone who asks receives, and the one who seeks finds, and to the one who knocks it will be opened. Or which one of you, if his son asks him for bread, will give him a stone? Or if he asks for a fish, will give him a serpent? If you then, who are evil, know how to give good gifts to your children, how much more will your Father who is in heaven give good things to those who ask him!" Matthew 7:7-11

## God wants me to pray for help when I am in trouble.

"And call upon me in the day of trouble; I will deliver you, and you shall glorify me." Psalm 50:15

From the end of the earth I call to you when my heart is faint. Lead me to the rock that is higher than I. Psalm 61:2

Contend, O LORD, with those who contend with me; fight against those who fight against me! Psalm 35:1

Let us then with confidence draw near to the throne of grace, that we may receive mercy and find grace to help in time of need. Hebrews 4:16

## God tells me some things he wants me to pray for.

Therefore pray earnestly to the Lord of the harvest to send out laborers into his harvest. Matthew 9:38

But I say to you, Love your enemies and pray for those who persecute you. Matthew 5:44

A
B
C
D
E
F
G
H
I
J
K
L
M
N
O
P
Q
R
S
T
U
V
W
X
Y
Z

**Jesus gave an example of how to pray.**
Pray then like this: "Our Father in heaven, hallowed be your name. Your kingdom come, your will be done, on earth as it is in heaven. Give us this day our daily bread, and forgive us our debts, as we also have forgiven our debtors. And lead us not into temptation, but deliver us from evil."
Matthew 6:9-13

Read some prayers that Paul prayed for his friends. Philippians 1:9-11; Colossians 1:9-11

John recorded a prayer Jesus prayed for me, in John 17:1-26. See verse 20

Rhoda was a little girl who prayed with her church that Peter would be released from jail. When God answered their prayers and Peter showed up, nobody in the church believed it was Peter except Rhoda! Acts 12:5-16

# PRIDE

Related topic: Humility

### I learn to stop being prideful as I learn to know God.

Talk no more so very proudly, let not arrogance come from your mouth; for the LORD is a God of knowledge, and by him actions are weighed. 1 Samuel 2:3

In the pride of his face the wicked does not seek him; all his thoughts are, "There is no God." Psalm 10:4

And I said: "Woe is me! For I am lost; for I am a man of unclean lips, and I dwell in the midst of a people of unclean lips; for my eyes have seen the King, the LORD of hosts!" Isaiah 6:5

### Because God hates pride, I am learning to hate it too!

There are six things that the LORD hates, seven that are an abomination to him: haughty eyes, a lying tongue, and hands that shed innocent blood, a heart that devises wicked plans, feet that make haste to run to evil, a false witness who breathes out lies, and one who sows discord among brothers. Proverbs 6:16-19

Pride and arrogance and the way of evil and perverted speech I hate. Proverbs 8:13b

For all that is in the world—the desires of the flesh and the desires of the eyes and pride in possessions—is not from the Father but is from the world. 1 John 2:16

Pride goes before destruction, and a haughty spirit before a fall. Proverbs 16:18

**God helps me fight pride by listening carefully.**

By insolence comes nothing but strife, but with those who take advice is wisdom. Proverbs 13:10

The way of a fool is right in his own eyes, but a wise man listens to advice. Proverbs 12:15

**God helps me fight pride by looking for wisdom and seeking God.**

When pride comes, then comes disgrace, but with the humble is wisdom. Proverbs 11:2

**God helps me fight pride by stopping wrong thoughts and starting to think right thoughts.**

For from within, out of the heart of man, come evil thoughts, sexual immorality, theft, murder, adultery, coveting, wickedness, deceit, sensuality, envy, slander, pride, foolishness. Mark 7:21-22

We destroy arguments and every lofty opinion raised against the knowledge of God, and take every thought captive to obey Christ. 2 Corinthians 10:5

**God helps me fight pride by loving others.**

This "knowledge" puffs up, but love builds up.
1 Corinthians 8:1

Therefore let anyone who thinks that he stands take heed lest he fall. 1 Corinthians 10:12

**God helps me fight pride by serving others, and not comparing myself with others.**

And they came to Capernaum. And when he [Jesus] was in the house he asked them, "What were you discussing on the way?" But they kept silent, for on the way they had argued with one another about who was the greatest. And he sat down and called the twelve. And he said to them, "If anyone would be first, he must be last of all and servant of all." Mark 9:33-35

## God helps me fight pride by becoming thankful.

For although they knew God, they did not honor him as God or give thanks to him, but they became futile in their thinking, and their foolish hearts were darkened. Claiming to be wise, they became fools. Romans 1:21-22

## God helps me fight pride by submitting to authority.

But he gives more grace. Therefore it says, "God opposes the proud, but gives grace to the humble." Submit yourselves therefore to God. Resist the devil, and he will flee from you. Draw near to God, and he will draw near to you. Cleanse your hands, you sinners, and purify your hearts, you double-minded. James 4:6-8

> King Nebuchadnezzar thought his success was all because he was so wonderful, but God caused him to lose his mind and act like an animal until he repented. Daniel 4:30-37
>
> For more reading about humility, read Philippians 2:3-11.
>
> Satan used to be an important angel who served God in Heaven. His pride caused him to rebel against God. Isaiah 14:12-15

A
B
C
D
E
F
G
H
I
J
K
L
M
N
O
P
Q
R
S
T
U
V
W
X
Y
Z

# PURITY

Even a child makes himself known by his acts, by whether his conduct is pure and upright. Proverbs 20:11

**Because God has saved me, and is making me pure like Jesus, he wants me to care about keeping my heart clean from sin.**

Beloved, we are God's children now, and what we will be has not yet appeared; but we know that when he appears we shall be like him, because we shall see him as he is. And everyone who thus hopes in him purifies himself as he is pure. 1 John 3:2-3

### I learn to be pure when I obey the Bible

How can a young man keep his way pure? By guarding it according to your word. Psalm 119:9

### I learn to be pure by keeping my thoughts right.

Keep your heart with all vigilance, for from it flow the springs of life. Proverbs 4:23

Finally, brothers, whatever is true, whatever is honorable, whatever is just, whatever is pure, whatever is lovely, whatever is commendable, if there is any excellence, if there is anything worthy of praise, think about these things. Philippians 4:8

We destroy arguments and every lofty opinion raised against the knowledge of God, and take every thought captive to obey Christ. 2 Corinthians 10:5

### I learn to be pure by avoiding sin.

I will not set before my eyes anything that is worthless. I hate the work of those who fall away; it shall not cling to me. Psalm 101:3

But Daniel resolved that he would not defile himself with the king's food, or with the wine that he drank. Therefore he asked the chief of the eunuchs to allow him not to defile himself. Daniel 1:8

And I find something more bitter than death: the woman whose heart is snares and nets, and whose hands are fetters. He who pleases God escapes her, but the sinner is taken by her. Ecclesiastes 7:26

**I learn to be pure by becoming wise!**
For the commandment is a lamp and the teaching a light, and the reproofs of discipline are the way of life, to preserve you from the evil woman, from the smooth tongue of the adulteress. Proverbs 6:23-24

# Rain

Are there any among the false gods of the nations that can bring rain? Or can the heavens give showers? Are you not he, O LORD our God? We set our hope on you, for you do all these things. Jeremiah 14:22

He loads the thick cloud with moisture; the clouds scatter his lightning. They turn around and around by his guidance, to accomplish all that he commands them on the face of the habitable world. Whether for correction or for his land or for love, he causes it to happen. Job 37:11-13

He [Jesus] answered them, "When it is evening, you say, 'It will be fair weather, for the sky is red.' And in the morning, 'It will be stormy today, for the sky is red and threatening.' You know how to interpret the appearance of the sky, but you cannot interpret the signs of the times." Matthew 16:2-3

A B C D E F G H I J K L M N O P Q R S T U V W X Y Z

# Rejection

Related topic: Lonely

## Sometimes friends act like enemies and reject us.

For it is not an enemy who taunts me—then I could bear it; it is not an adversary who deals insolently with me—then I could hide from him. But it is you, a man, my equal, my companion, my familiar friend. We used to take sweet counsel together; within God's house we walked in the throng. Psalm 55:12-14

## Sometimes we feel lonely when friends reject us.

My friends and companions stand aloof from my plague, and my nearest kin stand far off. Psalm 38:11

At my first defense no one came to stand by me, but all deserted me. May it not be charged against them! 2 Timothy 4:16

## Jesus tells me not to worry about being rejected, because he will never reject me.

"Blessed are you when people hate you and when they exclude you and revile you and spurn your name as evil, on account of the Son of Man!" Luke 6:22

"And wherever they do not receive you, when you leave that town shake off the dust from your feet as a testimony against them." Luke 9:5

What then shall we say to these things? If God is for us, who can be against us? Romans 8:31

For my father and my mother have forsaken me, but the LORD will take me in. Psalm 27:10

The Lord will rescue me from every evil deed and bring me safely into his heavenly kingdom. To him be the glory forever and ever. Amen. 2 Timothy 4:18

# REMEMBER

Related topic: Forget

## Remembering helps me do right!

Some trust in chariots and some in horses, but we trust in the name of the LORD our God. Psalm 20:7

So if you are offering your gift at the altar and there remember that your brother has something against you, leave your gift there before the altar and go. First be reconciled to your brother, and then come and offer your gift. Matthew 5:23-24

Remember also your Creator in the days of your youth, before the evil days come and the years draw near of which you will say, "I have no pleasure in them"; Ecclesiastes 12:1

## Meditating about what I remember helps me not to forget.

My soul will be satisfied as with fat and rich food, and my mouth will praise you with joyful lips, when I remember you upon my bed, and meditate on you in the watches of the night; Psalm 63:5-6

I remember the days of old; I meditate on all that you have done; I ponder the work of your hands. I stretch out my hands to you; my soul thirsts for you like a parched land. Selah Psalm 143:5-6

This Book of the Law shall not depart from your mouth, but you shall meditate on it day and night, so that you may be careful to do according to all that is written in it. For then you will make your way prosperous, and then you will have good success. Joshua 1:8

## Talking about what I remember helps me not to forget.

I will cause your name to be remembered in all generations; therefore nations will praise you forever and ever. Psalm 45:17

A B C D E F G H I J K L M N O P Q R S T U V W X Y Z

# REPENTANCE

Related topic: Sin

**The angels in heaven rejoice when I repent!**

"Just so, I tell you, there is joy before the angels of God over one sinner who repents." Luke 15:10

**When I see how loving and patient God is, I want to repent!**

Or do you presume on the riches of his kindness and forbearance and patience, not knowing that God's kindness is meant to lead you to repentance? Romans 2:4

Let the wicked forsake his way, and the unrighteous man his thoughts; let him return to the LORD, that he may have compassion on him, and to our God, for he will abundantly pardon. Isaiah 55:7

**God promises that he will always forgive me when I repent!**

If we confess our sins, he is faithful and just to forgive us our sins and to cleanse us from all unrighteousness. 1 John 1:9

Whoever conceals his transgressions will not prosper, but he who confesses and forsakes them will obtain mercy. Proverbs 28:13

> For more reading about repentance, read Psalms 32 and 51. King David wrote these poems when he repented of his sin.
>
> Read some examples of people who repented: the whole church at Corinth (2 Corinthians 7:9-11); the prodigal son (Luke 15:11-32); Jonah (Jonah 1-4).

# Respect

## God wants me to respect my parents.

Children, obey your parents in the Lord, for this is right. "Honor your father and mother" (this is the first commandment with a promise), "that it may go well with you and that you may live long in the land." Ephesians 6:1-3

## God wants me to respect others.

Love one another with brotherly affection. Outdo one another in showing honor. Romans 12:10

Honor everyone. Love the brotherhood. Fear God. Honor the emperor. 1 Peter 2:17

Do nothing from rivalry or conceit, but in humility count others more significant than yourselves. Let each of you look not only to his own interests, but also to the interests of others. Philippians 2:3-4

> The Rechabites were praised for respecting their grandfather's instructions even after they were grown. Jeremiah 35:13-19
>
> Rehoboam did not respect the wise counsel of the older men, but instead followed the foolish counsel of his friends. 1 Kings 12

# SADNESS

Related topics: Disappointment, Prayer, Hope, Give Up, Worry

**All the solutions to my sadness will not last unless my hope is in God. (See Omniscience)**

Some trust in chariots and some in horses, but we trust in the name of the LORD our God. Psalm 20:7

From the end of the earth I call to you when my heart is faint. Lead me to the rock that is higher than I, for you have been my refuge, a strong tower against the enemy. Psalm 61:2-3

With my voice I cry out to the LORD; with my voice I plead for mercy to the LORD. I pour out my complaint before him; I tell my trouble before him. When my spirit faints within me, you know my way! Psalm 142:1-3a

**When I am sad, I am helped by remembering that God loves me. (See God, Hope)**

Casting all your anxieties on him, because he cares for you. 1 Peter 5:7

Are not five sparrows sold for two pennies? And not one of them is forgotten before God. Why, even the hairs of your head are all numbered. Fear not; you are of more value than many sparrows. Luke 12:6-7

"Blessed are those who mourn, for they shall be comforted." Matthew 5:4

**When I am sad, I am helped by remembering that God controls all things. (See Omnipotence, Disappointment)**

For not from the east or from the west and not from the wilderness comes lifting up, but it is God who executes judgment, putting down one and lifting up another. Psalm 75:6-7

And we know that for those who love God all things work together for good, for those who are called according to his purpose. Romans 8:28

**When I don't know why I am sad or cannot think of the words to pray, the Holy Spirit prays the right words for me! (See Prayer)**

Likewise the Spirit helps us in our weakness. For we do not know what to pray for as we ought, but the Spirit himself intercedes for us with groanings too deep for words. And he who searches hearts knows what is the mind of the Spirit, because the Spirit intercedes for the saints according to the will of God. Romans 8:26-27

Why are you cast down, O my soul, and why are you in turmoil within me? Hope in God; for I shall again praise him, my salvation... Deep calls to deep at the roar of your waterfalls; all your breakers and your waves have gone over me. By day the LORD commands his steadfast love, and at night his song is with me, a prayer to the God of my life. Psalm 42:5, 7-8

**Sometimes I am sad because I have been lazy or not doing right. I am helped when I do right. (See Work, Chores, Repentance, Sin)**

Slothfulness casts into a deep sleep, and an idle person will suffer hunger. Proverbs 19:15

Behold, what I have seen to be good and fitting is to eat and drink and find enjoyment in all the toil with which one toils under the sun the few days of his life that God has given him, for this is his lot. Ecclesiastes 5:18

A B C D E F G H I J K L M N O P Q R S T U V W X Y Z

Blessed is the one whose transgression is forgiven!
Psalm 32:1a

**When I feel like giving up, I am helped by remembering Jesus' example, and his faithfulness to finish his work in my life. (See Give Up, Hope)**

And I am sure of this, that he who began a good work in you will bring it to completion at the day of Jesus Christ. Philippians 1:6

Therefore, since we are surrounded by so great a cloud of witnesses, let us also lay aside every weight, and sin which clings so closely, and let us run with endurance the race that is set before us, looking to Jesus, the founder and perfecter of our faith, who for the joy that was set before him endured the cross, despising the shame, and is seated at the right hand of the throne of God. Hebrews 12:1-2

Jesus still felt sadness even though he was doing right. Mark 14:34-36

Elijah was sad because he felt like he was the only one doing right. He also wasn't eating or sleeping well. 1 Kings 19:3-6

Job didn't understand why God was allowing problems in his life. He was helped by learning more about God. Job 23:8-10, and chapters 38-41. See Job's answer to God in Job 42:5-6.

Jonah was sad and angry because he did not want to do right. God wanted him to repent. Jonah 4

# SALVATION .......................................

Related topics: Sin, Repentance

For by grace you have been saved through faith. And this is not your own doing; it is the gift of God, not a result of works, so that no one may boast. Ephesians 2:8-9

"For God so loved the world, that he gave his only Son, that whoever believes in him should not perish but have eternal life." John 3:16

And they said, "Believe in the Lord Jesus, and you will be saved, you and your household." Acts 16:31

Because, if you confess with your mouth that Jesus is Lord and believe in your heart that God raised him from the dead, you will be saved. For with the heart one believes and is justified, and with the mouth one confesses and is saved. Romans 10:9-10

**When God's children are saved, they tell others that God has saved them.**
So everyone who acknowledges me before men, I also will acknowledge before my Father who is in heaven. Matthew 10:32

**The angels in heaven see and are happy whenever a little child is saved!**
"Just so, I tell you, there is joy before the angels of God over one sinner who repents." Luke 15:10

**I am saved and kept saved by the power of God!**
All that the Father gives me will come to me, and whoever comes to me I will never cast out. John 6:37

But to all who did receive him, who believed in his name, he gave the right to become children of God. John 1:12

But I am not ashamed, for I know whom I have believed, and I am convinced that he is able to guard until that Day what has been entrusted to me. 2 Timothy 1:12b

And I am sure of this, that he who began a good work in you will bring it to completion at the day of Jesus Christ. Philippians 1:6

### A saved child knows that he is becoming more like Christ.

Beloved, we are God's children now, and what we will be has not yet appeared; but we know that when he appears we shall be like him, because we shall see him as he is. And everyone who thus hopes in him purifies himself as he is pure. 1 John 3:2-3

### God's Word teaches me that I will stay in his hands and love, no matter what.

My sheep hear my voice, and I know them, and they follow me. I give them eternal life, and they will never perish, and no one will snatch them out of my hand. John 10:27-28

No, in all these things we are more than conquerors through him who loved us. For I am sure that neither death nor life, nor angels nor rulers, nor things present nor things to come, nor powers, nor height nor depth, nor anything else in all creation, will be able to separate us from the love of God in Christ Jesus our Lord. Romans 8:37-39

### Having a clean conscience (finding forgiveness) helps me to be sure I am saved!

Let us draw near [to God] with a true heart in full assurance of faith, with our hearts sprinkled clean from an evil conscience and our bodies washed with pure water. Let us hold fast the confession of our hope without wavering, for he who promised is faithful. Hebrews 10:22-23

For this very reason, make every effort to supplement your faith with virtue, and virtue with knowledge, and knowledge with self-control, and self-control with steadfastness, and steadfastness with godliness, and godliness with brotherly affection, and brotherly affection with love. For if these qualities are yours and are increasing, they keep you from being ineffective or unfruitful in the knowledge of our Lord Jesus Christ. For whoever lacks these qualities is so nearsighted that he is blind, having forgotten that he was cleansed from his former sins. 2 Peter 1:5-9

# SCHOOL

**I can learn to be faithful by studying hard in school, even when school is difficult or boring.**

And he said to him, 'Well done, good servant! Because you have been faithful in a very little, you shall have authority over ten cities.' Luke 19:17

Do you see a man skillful in his work? He will stand before kings; he will not stand before obscure men. Proverbs 22:29

Do your best to present yourself to God as one approved, a worker who has no need to be ashamed, rightly handling the word of truth. 2 Timothy 2:15

Whoever loves discipline loves knowledge, but he who hates reproof is stupid. Proverbs 12:1

Whatever your hand finds to do, do it with your might, for there is no work or thought or knowledge or wisdom in Sheol [the grave], to which you are going. Ecclesiastes 9:10

**I am sometimes tired of studying, but the most important thing to learn is to fear God and obey him.**

"Only take care, and keep your soul diligently, lest you forget the things that your eyes have seen, and lest they depart from your heart all the days of your life. Make them known to your children and your children's children" Deuteronomy 4:9

My son, beware of anything beyond these. Of making many books there is no end, and much study is a weariness of the flesh. The end of the matter; all has been heard. Fear God and keep his commandments, for this is the whole duty of man. Ecclesiastes 12:12-13

> People in the Bible who used their education: Solomon (1 Kings 4:32-34); Paul (Acts 17:28 and 22:3); Ezra (Ezra 7:10); Moses (Acts 7:22)

# SELF-CONTROL

Related topics: Contentment, Listening, Patience, Selfish

### Self control comes from the Holy Spirit when I obey God's Word.

But the fruit of the Spirit is love, joy, peace, patience, kindness, goodness, faithfulness, gentleness, self-control; against such things there is no law. Galatians 5:22-23

### Self-control helps me avoid a lot of trouble!

A man without self-control is like a city broken into and left without walls. Proverbs 25:28

Whoever keeps his mouth and his tongue keeps himself out of trouble. Proverbs 21:23

If you have found honey, eat only enough for you, lest you have your fill of it and vomit it. Proverbs 25:16

Whoever is slow to anger is better than the mighty, and he who rules his spirit than he who takes a city. Proverbs 16:32

But all things should be done decently and in order. 1 Corinthians 14:40

### Learning self control takes God's work in my life as well as hard work!

For this very reason, make every effort to supplement your faith with virtue, and virtue with knowledge, and knowledge with self-control... 2 Peter 1:5-6a

Or do you not know that your body is a temple of the Holy Spirit within you, whom you have from God? You are not your own, for you were bought with a price. So glorify God in your body. 1 Corinthians 6:19-20

Put off your old self, which belongs to your former manner of life and is corrupt through deceitful desires, and to be renewed in the spirit of your minds, and to put on the new self, created after the likeness of God in true righteousness and holiness. Ephesians 4:22-24

### When I choose to be patient with God's timing, I am learning self-control.

Wait for the LORD; be strong, and let your heart take courage; wait for the LORD! Psalm 27:14

But do not overlook this one fact, beloved, that with the Lord one day is as a thousand years, and a thousand years as one day. 2 Peter 3:8

The Lord is not slow to fulfill his promise as some count slowness, but is patient toward you, not wishing that any should perish, but that all should reach repentance. 2 Peter 3:9

A
B
C
D
E
F
G
H
I
J
K
L
M
N
O
P
Q
R
**S**
T
U
V
W
X
Y
Z

# SELF ESTEEM

Related topics: Shy, Confidence

**God wants me to see myself truthfully.**

For by the grace given to me I say to everyone among you not to think of himself more highly than he ought to think, but to think with sober judgment, each according to the measure of faith that God has assigned. Romans 12:3

I praise you, for I am fearfully and wonderfully made. Wonderful are your works; my soul knows it very well. My frame was not hidden from you, when I was being made in secret, intricately woven in the depths of the earth. Your eyes saw my unformed substance; in your book were written, every one of them, the days that were formed for me, when as yet there was none of them. Psalm 139:14-16

**God will help me do ANYTHING he wants me to do.**

I can do all things through him who strengthens me. Philippians 4:13

**God wants me to pray and ask him for help when I need it.**

Let us then with confidence draw near to the throne of grace, that we may receive mercy and find grace to help in time of need. Hebrews 4:16

**God is powerful, and my weaknesses are no trouble for him.**

But he said to me, "My grace is sufficient for you, for my power is made perfect in weakness." Therefore I will boast all the more gladly of my weaknesses, so that the power of Christ may rest upon me. For the sake of Christ, then, I am content with weaknesses, insults, hardships, persecutions, and calamities. For when I am weak, then I am strong. 2 Corinthians 12:9-10

For I know the plans I have for you, declares the LORD, plans for welfare and not for evil, to give you a future and a hope. Jeremiah 29:11

His delight is not in the strength of the horse, nor his pleasure in the legs of a man, but the LORD takes pleasure in those who fear him, in those who hope in his steadfast love. Psalm 147:10-11

**Jesus shows me that he wants me to think about others more than myself.**

Do nothing from rivalry or conceit, but in humility count others more significant than yourselves. Let each of you look not only to his own interests, but also to the interests of others. Have this mind among yourselves, which is yours in Christ Jesus, who, though he was in the form of God, did not count equality with God a thing to be grasped, but made himself nothing, taking the form of a servant, being born in the likeness of men. And being found in human form, he humbled himself by becoming obedient to the point of death, even death on a cross. Philippians 2:3-8

# SELFISH

Related topics: Pride, Humility

**Jesus wants me to fight me-first attitudes by learning to serve others.**

And they came to Capernaum. And when he [Jesus] was in the house he asked them, "What were you discussing on the way?" But they kept silent, for on the way they had argued with one another about who was the greatest. And he sat down and called the twelve. And he said to them, "If anyone would be first, he must be last of all and servant of all." Mark 9:33-35

Do nothing from rivalry or conceit, but in humility count others more significant than yourselves. Let each of you look not only to his own interests, but also to the interests of others. Philippians 2:3-4

"Even as the Son of Man came not to be served but to serve, and to give his life as a ransom for many." Matthew 20:28

**God wants me to stop having a me-first attitude, and to help those who are weak.**

We who are strong have an obligation to bear with the failings of the weak, and not to please ourselves. Let each of us please his neighbor for his good, to build him up. For Christ did not please himself... Romans 15:1-3a

> For examples of people in the Bible who were selfish, read here: Ahab (1 Kings 21:1-19); Haman (Esther 6:6); Satan (Isaiah 14:12-14); Ananias and Sapphira (Acts 5:1-11).

# SHY
Related topics: Self Esteem, Confidence, Fear of God

**God wants even shy children to do good works that others can see!**

In the same way, let your light shine before others, so that they may see your good works and give glory to your Father who is in heaven. Matthew 5:16

**Because God made me, I do not have to be afraid of people.**

Now the word of the LORD came to me, saying, "Before I formed you in the womb I knew you, and before you were born I consecrated you; I appointed you a prophet to the nations." Then I said, "Ah, Lord GOD! Behold, I do not know how to speak, for I am only a youth." But the LORD said to me, "Do not say, 'I am only a youth'; for to all to whom I send you, you shall go, and whatever I command you, you shall speak. Do not be afraid of them, for I am with you to deliver you, declares the LORD." Jeremiah 1:4-8

But Moses said to the LORD, "Oh, my Lord, I am not eloquent, either in the past or since you have spoken to your servant, but I am slow of speech and of tongue." Then the LORD said to him, "Who has made man's mouth? Who makes him mute, or deaf, or seeing, or blind? Is it not I, the LORD? Now therefore go, and I will be with your mouth and teach you what you shall speak." Exodus 4:10-12

**Fear of what people think of us is a trap that we can avoid when we learn to trust and fear God.**

The fear of man lays a snare, but whoever trusts in the LORD is safe. Proverbs 29:25

When I am afraid, I put my trust in you. In God, whose word I praise, in God I trust; I shall not be afraid. What can flesh do to me? Psalm 56:3-4

In whom [Jesus] we have boldness and access with confidence through our faith in him. Ephesians 3:12

A
B
C
D
E
F
G
H
I
J
K
L
M
N
O
P
Q
R
**S**
T
U
V
W
X
Y
Z

# SIN

Related topics: Repentance, Salvation

**Sin is not living up to God's glory.**

For all have sinned and fall short of the glory of God.
Romans 3:23

Everyone who makes a practice of sinning also practices
lawlessness; sin is lawlessness. You know that he appeared to
take away sins, and in him there is no sin. 1 John 3:4-5

**Because God sees everything, I cannot hide my sin
from God.**

And be sure your sin will find you out. Numbers 32:23b

**When Christians sin, God helps them to make things
right with him again.**

If we say we have no sin, we deceive ourselves, and the truth
is not in us. If we confess our sins, he is faithful and just to
forgive us our sins and to cleanse us from all unrighteousness. 1 John 1:8-9

For the righteous falls seven times and rises again...
Proverbs 24:16a

The steps of a man are established by the LORD, when
he delights in his way; though he fall, he shall not be cast
headlong, for the LORD upholds his hand. Psalm 37:23-24

**God has given me tools to help me keep from sin.**

I have stored up your word in my heart, that I might not sin
against you. Psalm 119:11

Therefore, confess your sins to one another and pray for one
another, that you may be healed. The prayer of a righteous
person has great power as it is working. James 5:16

To put off your old self, which belongs to your former manner of life and is corrupt through deceitful desires, and to be renewed in the spirit of your minds, and to put on the new self, created after the likeness of God in true righteousness and holiness. Ephesians 4:22-24

### God always gives me a way to escape sin!
No temptation has overtaken you that is not common to man. God is faithful, and he will not let you be tempted beyond your ability, but with the temptation he will also provide the way of escape, that you may be able to endure it. 1 Corinthians 10:13

### God loves me and is quick to forgive me when i sin!
For you, O Lord, are good and forgiving, abounding in steadfast love to all who call upon you. Psalm 86:5

The LORD is merciful and gracious, slow to anger and abounding in steadfast love. Psalm 103:8

As far as the east is from the west, so far does he remove our transgressions from us. As a father shows compassion to his children, so the LORD shows compassion to those who fear him. Psalm 103:12-13

### God always forgives me when I ask him to.
If we confess our sins, he is faithful and just to forgive us our sins and to cleanse us from all unrighteousness. 1 John 1:9

Who is a God like you, pardoning iniquity and passing over transgression for the remnant of his inheritance? He does not retain his anger forever, because he delights in steadfast love. He will again have compassion on us; he will tread our iniquities underfoot. You will cast all our sins into the depths of the sea. Micah 7:18-19

Jesus was tempted, but did not sin. His example shows us that temptation is not the same as sinning. Matthew 4:1-11, 2 Corinthians 5:21

A B C D E F G H I J K L M N O P Q R S T U V W X Y Z

# SLEEP

**I am helped when I go to sleep by thinking about the wonderful works of God!**

In peace I will both lie down and sleep; for you alone, O LORD, make me dwell in safety. Psalm 4:8

By day the LORD commands his steadfast love, and at night his song is with me, a prayer to the God of my life. Psalm 42:8

My soul will be satisfied as with fat and rich food, and my mouth will praise you with joyful lips, when I remember you upon my bed, and meditate on you in the watches of the night; for you have been my help, and in the shadow of your wings I will sing for joy. Psalm 63:5-7

It is in vain that you rise up early and go late to rest, eating the bread of anxious toil; for he gives to his beloved sleep. Psalm 127:2

**Sleep can be a bad thing if it is too much or at the wrong time.**

He who gathers in summer is a prudent son, but he who sleeps in harvest is a son who brings shame. Proverbs 10:5

How long will you lie there, O sluggard? When will you arise from your sleep? A little sleep, a little slumber, a little folding of the hands to rest... Proverbs 6:9-10

**God never sleeps; he is always ready to help!**

I lift up my eyes to the hills. From where does my help come? My help comes from the LORD, who made heaven and earth. He will not let your foot be moved; he who keeps you will not slumber. Behold, he who keeps Israel will neither slumber nor sleep. Psalm 121:1-4

## Rest is a result of trust and obedience.

Be still before the LORD and wait patiently for him; fret not yourself over the one who prospers in his way, over the man who carries out evil devices! Psalm 37:7

Thus says the LORD: "Stand by the roads, and look, and ask for the ancient paths, where the good way is; and walk in it, and find rest for your souls. But they said, 'We will not walk in it.' " Jeremiah 16:16

"Come to me, all who labor and are heavy laden, and I will give you rest. Take my yoke upon you, and learn from me, for I am gentle and lowly in heart, and you will find rest for your souls. For my yoke is easy, and my burden is light." Matthew 11:28-30

> Even in Bible times people sometimes grew tired with long preaching. Eutychus fell asleep and fell out of a window! Acts 20:9-12

A
B
C
D
E
F
G
H
I
J
K
L
M
N
O
P
Q
R
S
T
U
V
W
X
Y
Z

# SPORTS

An athlete is not crowned unless he competes according to the rules. 2 Timothy 2:5

For by you I can run against a troop, and by my God I can leap over a wall. This God—his way is perfect; the word of the LORD proves true; he is a shield for all those who take refuge in him. Psalm 18:29-30

**The Bible teaches that being a Christian is like being in a race.**

Do you not know that in a race all the runners run, but only one receives the prize? So run that you may obtain it. Every athlete exercises self-control in all things. They do it to receive a perishable wreath, but we an imperishable. So I do not run aimlessly; I do not box as one beating the air. But I discipline my body and keep it under control, lest after preaching to others I myself should be disqualified.
1 Corinthians 9:24-27

**A good athlete (and a good Christian) learns when to forget about past failures and victories. Instead he thinks about the game he is playing now.**

Brothers, I do not consider that I have made it my own. But one thing I do: forgetting what lies behind and straining forward to what lies ahead, I press on toward the goal for the prize of the upward call of God in Christ Jesus. Philippians 3:13-14

## God rewards Christians who work patiently and don't give up!

I have fought the good fight, I have finished the race, I have kept the faith. Henceforth there is laid up for me the crown of righteousness, which the Lord, the righteous judge, will award to me on that Day, and not only to me but also to all who have loved his appearing. 2 Timothy 4:7-8

Therefore, since we are surrounded by so great a cloud of witnesses, let us also lay aside every weight, and sin which clings so closely, and let us run with endurance the race that is set before us, looking to Jesus, the founder and perfecter of our faith, who for the joy that was set before him endured the cross, despising the shame, and is seated at the right hand of the throne of God. Consider him who endured from sinners such hostility against himself, so that you may not grow weary or fainthearted. Hebrews 12:1-3

A B C D E F G H I J K L M N O P Q R S T U V W X Y Z

# STARS

**The stars show God's greatness and goodness.**

The heavens declare the glory of God, and the sky above proclaims his handiwork. Day to day pours out speech, and night to night reveals knowledge. There is no speech, nor are there words, whose voice is not heard. Psalm 19:1-3

**God is so big that he knows all the stars, and he also knows and cares when I am hurting.**

He heals the brokenhearted and binds up their wounds. He determines the number of the stars; he gives to all of them their names. Great is our Lord, and abundant in power; his understanding is beyond measure. Psalm 147:3-5

**I follow the creator of the stars.**

[God], who alone stretched out the heavens and trampled the waves of the sea; who made the Bear and Orion, the Pleiades and the chambers of the south; who does great things beyond searching out, and marvelous things beyond number. Job 9:8-10

He who made the Pleiades and Orion, and turns deep darkness into the morning and darkens the day into night, who calls for the waters of the sea and pours them out on the surface of the earth, the LORD is his name; Amos 5:8

# STEALING

Related topics: Giving, Work, Contentment

"You shall not steal; you shall not deal falsely; you shall not lie to one another." Leviticus 19:11

**A child who wants to stop stealing must learn to work and give to others.**

Let the thief no longer steal, but rather let him labor, doing honest work with his own hands, so that he may have something to share with anyone in need. Ephesians 4:28

**A child who wants to stop stealing must learn to change how he thinks, and be content!**

Incline my heart to your testimonies, and not to selfish gain! Psalm 119:36

Keep your life free from love of money, and be content with what you have, for he has said, "I will never leave you nor forsake you." Hebrews 13:5

And he said, "What comes out of a person is what defiles him. For from within, out of the heart of man, come evil thoughts, sexual immorality, theft, murder, adultery, coveting, wickedness, deceit, sensuality, envy, slander, pride, foolishness." Mark 7:20-22

# Suffering

**Because God cares for me, he will help me when I go through difficult things**

Fear not, for I am with you; be not dismayed, for I am your God; I will strengthen you, I will help you, I will uphold you with my righteous right hand. Isaiah 41:10

Casting all your anxieties on him, because he cares for you. 1 Peter 5:7

For I know the plans I have for you, declares the LORD, plans for welfare and not for evil, to give you a future and a hope. Jeremiah 29:11

**There will be no suffering in heaven.**

"[In heaven], He will wipe away every tear from their eyes, and death shall be no more, neither shall there be mourning, nor crying, nor pain anymore, for the former things have passed away." Revelation 21:4

We are afflicted in every way, but not crushed; perplexed, but not driven to despair; persecuted, but not forsaken; struck down, but not destroyed; always carrying in the body the death of Jesus, so that the life of Jesus may also be manifested in our bodies. 2 Corinthians 4:8-10

**God expects believers to treat children with kindness and respect.**

"Whoever receives one such child in my name receives me, but whoever causes one of these little ones who believe in me to sin, it would be better for him to have a great millstone fastened around his neck and to be drowned in the depth of the sea." Matthew 18:5-6

**Because God comforts me, I can be like him when I comfort others who are suffering too.**

[God] who comforts us in all our affliction, so that we may be able to comfort those who are in any affliction, with the comfort with which we ourselves are comforted by God. 2 Corinthians 1:4

So we do not lose heart. Though our outer self is wasting away, our inner self is being renewed day by day. For this light momentary affliction is preparing for us an eternal weight of glory beyond all comparison, as we look not to the things that are seen but to the things that are unseen. For the things that are seen are transient, but the things that are unseen are eternal. 2 Corinthians 4:16-18

**God loves me, even when I make wrong choices.**

Who shall separate us from the love of Christ? Shall tribulation, or distress, or persecution, or famine, or nakedness, or danger, or sword? As it is written, "For your sake we are being killed all the day long; we are regarded as sheep to be slaughtered." No, in all these things we are more than conquerors through him who loved us. For I am sure that neither death nor life, nor angels nor rulers, nor things present nor things to come, nor powers, nor height nor depth, nor anything else in all creation, will be able to separate us from the love of God in Christ Jesus our Lord. Romans 8:35-39

**Paul used the laws of Rome to protect himself.**

And the jailer reported these words to Paul, saying, "The magistrates have sent to let you go. Therefore come out now and go in peace." But Paul said to them, "They have beaten us publicly, uncondemned, men who are Roman citizens, and have thrown us into prison; and do they now throw us out secretly? No! Let them come themselves and take us out." The police reported these words to the magistrates, and they were afraid when they heard that they were Roman citizens. Acts 16:36-38

**God gave government and laws to punish evildoers and protect his children.**

Be subject for the Lord's sake to every human institution, whether it be to the emperor as supreme, or to governors as sent by him to punish those who do evil and to praise those who do good. 1 Peter 2:13-14

See also how Paul reported wrongdoing to the authorities to protect himself: Acts 23:16-35.

# TALKING

**Sometimes it is good to learn to be quiet!**

Whoever keeps his mouth and his tongue keeps himself out of trouble. Proverbs 21:23

And to aspire to live quietly, and to mind your own affairs, and to work with your hands, as we instructed you,
1 Thessalonians 4:11

Know this, my beloved brothers: let every person be quick to hear, slow to speak, slow to anger; James 1:19

When words are many, transgression is not lacking, but whoever restrains his lips is prudent. Proverbs 10:19

**God's children learn not to criticize others.**

Whoever belittles his neighbor lacks sense, but a man of understanding remains silent. Proverbs 11:12

**God's children learn to use words to encourage others.**

Anxiety in a man's heart weighs him down, but a good word makes him glad. Proverbs 12:25

Let no corrupting talk come out of your mouths, but only such as is good for building up, as fits the occasion, that it may give grace to those who hear. Ephesians 4:29

**The right word at the right time is beautiful.**
A word fitly spoken is like apples of gold in a setting of silver. Proverbs 25:11

To make an apt answer is a joy to a man, and a word in season, how good it is! Proverbs 15:23

The Preacher sought to find words of delight, and uprightly he wrote words of truth. The words of the wise are like goads, and like nails firmly fixed are the collected sayings; they are given by one Shepherd. Ecclesiastes 12:10-11

# TEASING

**Bad teasing makes others look foolish because they do not see or understand the joke.**
You shall not curse the deaf or put a stumbling block before the blind, but you shall fear your God: I am the LORD. Leviticus 19:14

**Bad teasing laughs at sin.**
Let there be no filthiness nor foolish talk nor crude joking, which are out of place, but instead let there be thanksgiving. Ephesians 5:4

**Bad teasing is hurtful. Saying "I'm just joking" doesn't make it okay.**
Like a madman who throws firebrands, arrows, and death is the man who deceives his neighbor and says, "I am only joking!" Proverbs 26:18-19

**Good teasing is kind, and enjoyed by both people.**
"So whatever you wish that others would do to you, do also to them, for this is the Law and the Prophets." Matthew 7:12

Let each of you look not only to his own interests, but also to the interests of others. Philippians 2:4

A joyful heart is good medicine, but a crushed spirit dries up the bones. Proverbs 17:22

**Good teasing is at the right time.**
[There is] a time to weep, and a time to laugh; a time to mourn, and a time to dance; Ecclesiastes 3:4

# THANKFULNESS

Give thanks in all circumstances; for this is the will of God in Christ Jesus for you. 1 Thessalonians 5:18

**One way I can say thank you to God is by telling my friends about God's goodness!**
I will sing of the steadfast love of the LORD, forever; with my mouth I will make known your faithfulness to all generations. Psalm 89:1

Rejoice in the LORD, O you righteous, and give thanks to his holy name! Psalm 97:12

**Godly people are thankful people.**
Let the word of Christ dwell in you richly, teaching and admonishing one another in all wisdom, singing psalms and hymns and spiritual songs, with thankfulness in your hearts to God. And whatever you do, in word or deed, do everything in the name of the Lord Jesus, giving thanks to God the Father through him. Colossians 3:16-17

**Because God loves me so much, I say thank you to God when I pray!**
Continue steadfastly in prayer, being watchful in it with thanksgiving. Colossians 4:2

Do not be anxious about anything, but in everything by prayer and supplication with thanksgiving let your requests be made known to God. Philippians 4:6

Through him then let us continually offer up a sacrifice of praise to God, that is, the fruit of lips that acknowledge his name. Hebrews 13:15

It is good to give thanks to the LORD, to sing praises to your name, O Most High; to declare your steadfast love in the morning, and your faithfulness by night, to the music of the lute and the harp, to the melody of the lyre. For you, O LORD, have made me glad by your work; at the works of your hands I sing for joy. Psalm 92:1-4

I will recount the steadfast love of the LORD, the praises of the LORD, according to all that the LORD has granted us, and the great goodness to the house of Israel that he has granted them according to his compassion, according to the abundance of his steadfast love. Isaiah 63:7

**King David shows me a good example to start my prayer and worship with thanksgiving and praise.**
Enter his gates with thanksgiving, and his courts with praise! Give thanks to him; bless his name! Psalm 100:4

Blessed be the Lord, who daily bears us up; God is our salvation. Selah Psalm 68:19

I will rejoice and be glad in your steadfast love, because you have seen my affliction; you have known the distress of my soul.  Psalm 31:7

Oh, how abundant is your goodness, which you have stored up for those who fear you and worked for those who take refuge in you, in the sight of the children of mankind! Psalm 31:19

# TRIAL / TROUBLE

See Suffering

# TRUST

Related topics: Faith, Omnipotence

Trust in the LORD with all your heart, and do not lean on your own understanding. In all your ways acknowledge him, and he will make straight your paths. Proverbs 3:5-6

For you, O Lord, are my hope, my trust, O LORD, from my youth. Psalm 71:5

## The power and goodness of God makes it so that I can trust him.

The LORD is my strength and my shield; in him my heart trusts, and I am helped; my heart exults, and with my song I give thanks to him. Psalm 28:7

This God—his way is perfect; the word of the LORD proves true; he is a shield for all those who take refuge in him. Psalm 18:30

## When I trust God, and he helps me, my heart sings for joy.

But let all who take refuge in you rejoice; let them ever sing for joy, and spread your protection over them, that those who love your name may exult in you. Psalm 5:11

Oh, taste and see that the LORD is good! Blessed is the man who takes refuge in him! Psalm 34:8

## Trusting things, people, and even myself, is foolish!

Whoever trusts in his riches will fall, but the righteous will flourish like a green leaf. Proverbs 11:28

Whoever trusts in his own mind is a fool, but he who walks in wisdom will be delivered. Proverbs 28:26

Thus says the LORD: "Cursed is the man who trusts in man and makes flesh his strength, whose heart turns away from the LORD." Jeremiah 17:5

# TRUTH TELLING

Related topic: Lying

**Because Jesus is truth, I must tell the truth to be right with God.**

Jesus said to him, "I am the way, and the truth, and the life. No one comes to the Father except through me." John 14:6

**God delights in us when we tell the truth!**

Lying lips are an abomination to the LORD, but those who act faithfully are his delight. Proverbs 12:22b

**King David prayed that God would help him to tell the truth.**

Put false ways far from me and graciously teach me your law! I have chosen the way of faithfulness; I set your rules before me. Psalm 119:29-30

Whoever conceals his transgressions will not prosper, but he who confesses and forsakes them will obtain mercy. Proverbs 28:13

**The person who is living truthfully loves to be near the light of God and his word. The person who lives a lie stays away from the light of God and his word.**

"For everyone who does wicked things hates the light and does not come to the light, lest his works should be exposed. But whoever does what is true comes to the light, so that it may be clearly seen that his works have been carried out in God." John 3:20-21

**When someone else is lying, I should remember that God sees all the secrets, and he reveals them in his time.**

Daniel answered and said: "Blessed be the name of God forever and ever, to whom belong wisdom and might. He changes times and seasons; he removes kings and sets up kings; he gives wisdom to the wise and knowledge to those who have understanding; he reveals deep and hidden things; he knows what is in the darkness, and the light dwells with him." Daniel 2:20-22

For I will proclaim the name of the LORD; ascribe greatness to our God! "The Rock, his work is perfect, for all his ways are justice. A God of faithfulness and without iniquity, just and upright is he." Deuteronomy 32:3-4

# WAR

Related topic: Suffering

**Fights and wars are bad. They come from selfish and prideful desires.**

By insolence comes nothing but strife, but with those who take advice is wisdom. Proverbs 13:10

What causes quarrels and what causes fights among you? Is it not this, that your passions are at war within you? You desire and do not have, so you murder. You covet and cannot obtain, so you fight and quarrel. You do not have, because you do not ask. James 4:1-2

**God's people sometimes learn to use weapons, but they ask God to protect them.**

For not in my bow do I trust, nor can my sword save me. But you have saved us from our foes and have put to shame those who hate us. Psalm 44:6-7

Blessed be the LORD, my rock, who trains my hands for war, and my fingers for battle; he is my steadfast love and my fortress, my stronghold and my deliverer, my shield and he in whom I take refuge, who subdues peoples under me. Psalm 144:1-2

Woe to those who go down to Egypt for help and rely on horses, who trust in chariots because they are many and in horsemen because they are very strong, but do not look to the Holy One of Israel or consult the LORD! Isaiah 31:1

### God shows his power by creating Leviathan, who was not threatened by the weapons of men.

Though the sword reaches him, it does not avail, nor the spear, the dart, or the javelin. He counts iron as straw, and bronze as rotten wood. The arrow cannot make him flee; for him sling stones are turned to stubble. Clubs are counted as stubble; he laughs at the rattle of javelins. Job 41:26-29

### God is my commander in chief, and my job is to please him in spiritual battle.

Share in suffering as a good soldier of Christ Jesus. No soldier gets entangled in civilian pursuits, since his aim is to please the one who enlisted him. 2 Timothy 2:3-4

Therefore take up the whole armor of God, that you may be able to withstand in the evil day, and having done all, to stand firm. Stand therefore, having fastened on the belt of truth, and having put on the breastplate of righteousness, and, as shoes for your feet, having put on the readiness given by the gospel of peace. In all circumstances take up the shield of faith, with which you can extinguish all the flaming darts of the evil one; and take the helmet of salvation, and the sword of the Spirit, which is the word of God. Ephesians 6:13-17

A
B
C
D
E
F
G
H
I
J
K
L
M
N
O
P
Q
R
S
T
U
V
**W**
X
Y
Z

King David was a warrior who loved and served God. 1 Samuel 17:49-51

Read about other skilled warriors that served God. 1 Chronicles 12:1-3, 12:8-15

The Centurion was a soldier of great faith. Luke 7:2-9

# WILL OF GOD

Related topic: Wisdom

**Because God has changed my heart, I want to do his will!**

You have multiplied, O LORD my God, your wondrous deeds and your thoughts toward us; none can compare with you! I will proclaim and tell of them, yet they are more than can be told... I delight to do your will, O my God; your law is within my heart. Psalm 40:5, 8

**Wisdom helps me to know God's will.**

Therefore do not be foolish, but understand what the will of the Lord is. Ephesians 5:17

**Because God is kind and loves me, I trust he will answer me when I pray and ask him about his will.**

Let me hear in the morning of your steadfast love, for in you I trust. Make me know the way I should go, for to you I lift up my soul. Psalm 143:8

Teach me to do your will, for you are my God! Let your good Spirit lead me on level ground! Psalm 143:10

Trust in the LORD with all your heart, and do not lean on your own understanding. In all your ways acknowledge him, and he will make straight your paths. Proverbs 3:5-6

**God's will is for me to obey with the right attitude!**
Slaves, obey your earthly masters with fear and trembling, with a sincere heart, as you would Christ, not by the way of eye-service, as people-pleasers, but as servants of Christ, doing the will of God from the heart. Ephesians 6:5-6

Give thanks in all circumstances; for this is the will of God in Christ Jesus for you. 1 Thessalonians 5:18

**Because God is merciful, he changes me. Then I can find God's will by filling my mind with good things.**
I appeal to you therefore, brothers, by the mercies of God, to present your bodies as a living sacrifice, holy and acceptable to God, which is your spiritual worship. Do not be conformed to this world, but be transformed by the renewal of your mind, that by testing you may discern what is the will of God, what is good and acceptable and perfect. Romans 12:1-2

# WISDOM
Related topic: Will of God

**God loves to give wisdom, and he wants me to ask him for it!**
If any of you lacks wisdom, let him ask God, who gives generously to all without reproach, and it will be given him. James 1:5

**Wisdom is better than anything I could ever want!**
For wisdom is better than jewels, and all that you may desire cannot compare with her. Proverbs 8:11

A
B
C
D
E
F
G
H
I
J
K
L
M
N
O
P
Q
R
S
T
U
V
W
X
Y
Z

My son, eat honey, for it is good, and the drippings of the honeycomb are sweet to your taste. Know that wisdom is such to your soul; if you find it, there will be a future, and your hope will not be cut off. Proverbs 24:13-14

**Jesus teaches that the way to be wise is to hear God's Word, and also obey it.**
"Everyone then who hears these words of mine and does them will be like a wise man who built his house on the rock." Matthew 7:24

The fear of the LORD is the beginning of wisdom; all those who practice it have a good understanding. His praise endures forever! Psalm 111:10

**Learning God's words without obeying them is not wise. It is foolish!**
And everyone who hears these words of mine and does not do them will be like a foolish man who built his house on the sand. Matthew 7:26

**King Solomon wrote the book of Proverbs so children like me could learn to be wise.**
The proverbs of Solomon, son of David, king of Israel: To know wisdom and instruction, to understand words of insight... Proverbs 1:1-2

**Fake wisdom might sound good, but it looks bad.**
But if you have bitter jealousy and selfish ambition in your hearts, do not boast and be false to the truth. This is not the wisdom that comes down from above, but is earthly, unspiritual, demonic. For where jealousy and selfish ambition exist, there will be disorder and every vile practice. James 3:14-16

**True wisdom isn't just good words. It results in good actions, too.**

But the wisdom from above is first pure, then peaceable, gentle, open to reason, full of mercy and good fruits, impartial and sincere. And a harvest of righteousness is sown in peace by those who make peace. James 3:17-18

> When God told Solomon to make a wish for whatever he wanted, Solomon asked for wisdom. 1 Kings 3:5-10
>
> God was so pleased that he made Solomon the wisest man who ever lived. 1 Kings 4:29-34

# WORK
...............................................

Related Topics: Chores, School, Give Up

Whatever you do, work heartily, as for the Lord and not for men. Colossians 3:23

**God created my body and mind to be able to work. Work is a blessing, and not a curse!**

There is nothing better for a person than that he should eat and drink and find enjoyment in his toil. This also, I saw, is from the hand of God. Ecclesiastes 2:24

The LORD God took the man [Adam] and put him in the garden of Eden to work it and keep it. Genesis 2:15

A B C D E F G H I J K L M N O P Q R S T U V W X Y Z

### God uses the ant to teach me how to work hard without being told.

Go to the ant, O sluggard; consider her ways, and be wise. Without having any chief, officer, or ruler, she prepares her bread in summer and gathers her food in harvest.
Proverbs 6:6-8

### God wants me to learn diligent and honest work.

And to aspire to live quietly, and to mind your own affairs, and to work with your hands, as we instructed you, so that you may walk properly before outsiders and be dependent on no one. 1 Thessalonians 4:11-12

Do you see a man skillful in his work? He will stand before kings; he will not stand before obscure men. Proverbs 22:29

### Lazy people make excuses instead of working.

The sluggard does not plow in the autumn; he will seek at harvest and have nothing. Proverbs 20:4

The sluggard says, "There is a lion outside! I shall be killed in the streets!" Proverbs 22:13

### God has chosen work to provide for my needs.

For even when we were with you, we would give you this command: If anyone is not willing to work, let him not eat. For we hear that some among you walk in idleness, not busy at work, but busybodies. Now such persons we command and encourage in the Lord Jesus Christ to do their work quietly and to earn their own living. As for you, brothers, do not grow weary in doing good.
2 Thessalonians 3:10-13

Whoever is slothful will not roast his game, but the diligent man will get precious wealth.
Proverbs 12:27

## God rested after he worked, and wants me to rest after I work!

And on the seventh day God finished his work that he had done, and he rested on the seventh day from all his work that he had done. So God blessed the seventh day and made it holy, because on it God rested from all his work that he had done in creation. Genesis 2:2-3

## God sees and rewards the hard work of his children.

Therefore, my beloved brothers, be steadfast, immovable, always abounding in the work of the Lord, knowing that in the Lord your labor is not in vain. 1 Corinthians 15:58

For God is not unjust so as to overlook your work and the love that you have shown for his name in serving the saints, as you still do. And we desire each one of you to show the same earnestness to have the full assurance of hope until the end, so that you may not be sluggish, but imitators of those who through faith and patience inherit the promises. Hebrews 6:10-12

A
B
C
D
E
F
G
H
I
J
K
L
M
N
O
P
Q
R
S
T
U
V
W
X
Y
Z

# WORRY

Related topic: Afraid

Therefore do not be anxious, saying, 'What shall we eat?' or 'What shall we drink?' or 'What shall we wear?' For the Gentiles seek after all these things, and your heavenly Father knows that you need them all. Matthew 6:31-32

But seek first the kingdom of God and his righteousness, and all these things will be added to you. Therefore do not be anxious about tomorrow, for tomorrow will be anxious for itself. Sufficient for the day is its own trouble. Matthew 6:33-34

It is in vain that you rise up early and go late to rest, eating the bread of anxious toil; for he gives to his beloved sleep. Psalm 127:2

## When I worry, God teaches me to pray.

Do not be anxious about anything, but in everything by prayer and supplication with thanksgiving let your requests be made known to God. And the peace of God, which surpasses all understanding, will guard your hearts and your minds in Christ Jesus. Philippians 4:6-7

## God's Children learn to think about good things instead of worry!

Finally, brothers, whatever is true, whatever is honorable, whatever is just, whatever is pure, whatever is lovely, whatever is commendable, if there is any excellence, if there is anything worthy of praise, think about these things. What you have learned and received and heard and seen in me— practice these things, and the God of peace will be with you. Philippians 4:8-9

# ZEAL

## Good zeal is energy and eagerness to do right.

Now I urge you, brothers—you know that the household of Stephanas were the first converts in Achaia, and that they have devoted themselves to the service of the saints—
1 Corinthians 16:15

Waiting for our blessed hope, the appearing of the glory of our great God and Savior Jesus Christ, who gave himself for us to redeem us from all lawlessness and to purify for himself a people for his own possession who are zealous for good works. Titus 2:13-14

King Josiah had zeal to do right, even when he was only eight years old! God blessed his tender and humble heart. II Chronicles 34

God used Nehemiah to share his zeal to rebuild the temple! Nehemiah 2:17-20

# 10 Ways to Use the Book

- *Topical Bible for Kids* can be used as a tool for family devotions. Children or parents can pick a topic for discussion, and then read, discuss, or memorize the verses for that topic together. Any of the following recommendations can also be implemented as hands-on family devotion activities.

- My friend Emily secretly chooses a topic, does a sword drill of the references with her children, and has them guess the topic. Then they discuss the verses. (This is a great way to use the book with different Bible translations.)

- During mealtime discussions or car trips, ask children to identify topics and verses that they like. I like to ask, "What is God teaching you? What are your favorite verses on that topic?" Sometimes I bring up a topic to start the conversation: "What verses comfort you when you are sad?" "Would you like to find some verses together that will be a help to you?" These questions and follow-up study help them see that the Bible is an enjoyable resource for life and delight, and not a club of punishment.

- Using this book as a starting point, help children write out favorite verses in a handmade book, or on index cards to tape on their wall next to their beds. They may enjoy making and printing "business cards" with topics, verses, and clip art. These also make good gifts.

- Help young children find and highlight verses they have memorized. These are the easiest verses for new and struggling readers to find in the Bible and read. Read the topics from the table of contents and ask them to stop you when they are interested in finding verses on that topic. Then, encourage them to highlight their favorite verses in their Bibles.

- Consider allowing children to stay up late, if they are reading or listening to their Bible in their rooms. Teach them that a child doesn't have to be a good reader to love and obey the Bible!

- If children are looking for topics not included in this book, show them how to search for new topics online (such as at biblegateway.com), or with a concordance. Help them collect verses on their interests.

- Help children make a chain of verses in their Bibles by writing the next reference on a topic in the margin. Making connections is one way children (and parents) learn to be active and happy students of God's Word.

- Help children identify Bible synonyms and key words for topics by circling the words in the text that correspond to the topic. (For example, in the topic "Fighting," Bible words include strife, wars, contention.)

- Help children identify Bible opposites as they study: fighting and forgiveness, complain and contentment, and so on. Many opposites are already given as cross references in the text.

This book is a gift to my three children: David, Bethel, and Laurel, with the prayer that they continue to learn to love God and His Word with all their hearts.

Thank you to my husband, Lee, who has encouraged me and supported me throughout this project. He is the one who pushed me to invest in new software, who helped me over the initial shock of learning a new program, language and procedures, and who solved the really big problems when I got stuck. He brought home red licorice and gummi bears many times and kept up the supply of fresh roasted coffee in spite of his own busy schedule. Thank you for making this book possible!

Thank you to my brother Thomas Pryde, and Jay Younts, for their encouragement, and the hours they gave providing theological feedback for this project.

Thank you also to Laura Weimer, Deborah Hawkins, Denise Franklin, Emily Helmick, and others who read early versions and gave valuable feedback from a mother's perspective.

I am also grateful to my parents, who have shown me all my life what it looks like to delight in God and his word.

*We will not hide them from their children,*
*but tell to the coming generation*
*the glorious deeds of the LORD, and his might,*
*and the wonders that he has done.*
*He established a testimony in Jacob*
*and appointed a law in Israel,*
*which he commanded our fathers*
*to teach to their children,*
*that the next generation might know them,*
*the children yet unborn,*
*and arise and tell them to their children, so that*
*they should set their hope in God*
*and not forget the works of God,*
*but keep his commandments;*

*Psalm 78:4-7*

85913660R00093

Made in the USA
Lexington, KY
06 April 2018